Death of a Cruise Ship

CAPITAL BOOKS
23 Waring-Taylor St
Box 5534, WELLINGTON
Ph 473 9358 Fax 472 3163

Death of a Cruise Ship
The Mystery of the Mikhail Lermontov

Tom O'Connor

CAPE CATLEY LTD

First published 1999

CAPE CATLEY LTD
Whatamango Bay, Queen Charlotte Sound,
New Zealand
e-mail: cape.catley@xtra.co.nz

Copyright © Tom O'Connor 1999

This book is copyright under the Berne Convention
All rights reserved
No reproduction without permission
Enquiries should be made to the publishers

Cover design by Bill Wieben
Typeset by PK Publications, Picton
Printed in Hong Kong
Cover photograph courtesy Les Goss, CTC.
(Within 16 hours of this photo of the *Mikhail Lermontov*
being taken, she was lying on the bottom of the sea.)

ISBN: 0-908561-69-5

Dedicated to
Parvee Zagliadimov
1951 Moscow, USSR - 1986 Port Gore, New Zealand
and to the many rescuers, both New Zealand and Russian,
who by their courage prevented what could have been the
greatest disaster in New Zealand's maritime history.

Contents

	Page
Author's Note and Acknowledgements	6

PART ONE

Chapter 1 - In Picton	9
Chapter 2 - The Decision	25
Chapter 3 - The Rocks	41
Chapter 4 - Rescuers Gather	51
Chapter 5 - "Assistance Not Required"	69
Chapter 6 - Terror in the Darkness	78
Chapter 7 - Death Throes of a Ship	98
Chapter 8 - Wellington	111

PART TWO

Chapter 9 - Captain Ponsford Investigates	130
Chapter 10 - Diving Deep	154
Chapter 11 - A Political Cover-Up?	165
Chapter 12 - Death Throes of a Harbour Board	174
Chapter 13 - Final Moves	186
Epilogue	195
Bibliography	199
Glossary	200

Author's Note

When I joined *The Marlborough Express* as a journalist towards the end of 1987 I was stationed in Picton. There one of my duties was to attend and report on meetings of the Marlborough Harbour Board which was enmeshed in the complex aftermath of the sinking of the *Mikhail Lermontov*. This cruise ship had gone down in Port Gore in the outer Marlborough Sounds at the beginning of the previous year.

In 1996, to mark the tenth anniversary of the loss of the ship, my editor, Brendon Burns, asked me to write a three-part feature on the event, which at that time was still shrouded in mystery and rumour. During my research for the feature it became apparent that the actual story behind the loss of the ship was much more complex and fascinating than anyone had ever imagined.

Soon after publication of this feature I was speaking with Christine Cole Catley, who had established *The Picton Paper*, and is the founder and editor of the publishing firm, Cape Catley, in the Marlborough Sounds. She told me she had already declined two or three part-manuscripts on the *Mikhail Lermontov*; they didn't tell the human story. As it was obvious books would appear sooner or later, we decided I would build on my initial research, focusing where possible on the personal experiences of passengers, crew and rescuers, and the framework of the whole event including the political developments both before and after the tragedy. We would try to find out not only what people did, but what they thought and felt.

My task was to seek out the truth from the web of rumour, myth and secrecy which had entangled the ship, the Marlborough Harbour Board and the New Zealand Government from the day of the sinking a decade earlier. Most importantly we would publish what Chris Cole Catley called the 'compassionate truth'. There had been enough accusation, recrimination and litigation. I was seeking the human story of what happened.

In spite of what I and others already knew about the loss of the *Mikhail Lermonto*, I was amazed at what I discovered when I began interviewing so many of the people involved.

I have read hundreds of documents from Australia, Russia and from within New Zealand, and checked several thousand pages of so-called 'closed files'. Learning where and how to look took a great deal of time and patience.

The full proceedings from the Ponsford Enquiry were made available to me from several sources. A huge amount of material had to be checked and re-checked for accuracy and reliability. The result is a sad story of petty political intrigue in 1980s' New Zealand, but also a gripping tale of bravery in the best tradition of ships and seafarers. None of the information uncovered during several years of investigation for this book was provided by the Marlborough District Council or the former Marlborough Harbour Board. Their files remain closed.

This book represents the combined stories of hundreds of people who gave their individual memories of one of the most controversial and mysterious shipwrecks of modern times.

I am particularly indebted to Captain John Brew (now master of the Interislander ferry *Arahura*), Captain Vladislav Vorobyov (master of the freight ship *Udong*, formerly master of the *Mikhail Lermontov*), Captain Steve Ponsford, Inspector of Ships), Captain John Reedman of the *Tarihiko*, and Captain James Gray (Marine Surveyor, Australia). Their personal recollections of the disaster which befell the *Mikhail Lermontov* and their professional knowledge make up the essential core of the story.

My two former editors, Reg Spowart and Brendon Burns, gave me the time to research the histories of the Marlborough Harbour Board and the *Mikhail Lermontov* during my nine years with *The Marlborough Express* newspaper. George Richards of the *Sydney Morning Herald* gave assistance in making contact with Australian passengers.

Tracey Sutherland (Australian correspondent, Moscow) helped with making contact with Captain Vorobyov. Olga Korobtseva (language translator, Moscow) gave much assistance with interviews. I particularly needed to know not just what Captain Vorobyov did and said, but what he thought and felt, as the drama unfolded.

Richard Prebble MP, now leader of ACT and a former Labour Minister of Transport, gave previously unpublished political details. Kennedy Warne, editor of the *New Zealand Geographic*, and Ray O'Neill were particularly generous with photographic assistance. Ray Hatch and others also gave details of the dangers of diving on the ship.

I am grateful to the many passengers who shared their memories. Particularly I thank Joan Dillon, Mark Raymond, Barbara Powell, Jean and Harry Thomas, Robert and Enid Diffin, Wal and Jean Thorpe, Ray and Lorna Leihn and their grandsons John and Steven, Tom and Dorothy Archer, Sheila Simpson, Heather Steel, Lorand Loblay and Noeline Rodger. They gave chilling and very personal insights into the terrors of the shipwreck. Entertainment officers on the ship, such as Lee Young and Bunny Gibson, managed to provide some humour with their memories. Among the rescuers, fishermen and other Sounds people such as David Baker were generous with their memories.

Thanks, too, to Pauline Summerville, for word processing assistance; Graham and Cynthia Brooks, for technical advice and encouragement; Dick Challis for technical assistance with the photographs; Migs Eder and Julie Clifton for valuable additional research; Christine Cole Catley for her very considerable contribution of research, writing and checking; and finally thanks to my wife, Joy, a literary critic without peer or pity.

Tom O'Connor
March 1999

PART ONE

CHAPTER ONE

In Picton

THE brilliant white hull of the cruise ship *Mikhail Lermontov* stood out sharply against the grey-green sea and the cloud-muffled sky as early morning found her out in Cook Strait. It was 16 February 1986.

Somewhere, hidden in the cliffs which loomed directly ahead, was the narrow entrance to Tory Channel in the outer Marlborough Sounds, the channel the ship would follow to reach Picton.

At 20,000 tonnes she was one of the bigger vessels scheduled to visit this small port at the top of the South Island. She was to be in the vanguard of an increased emphasis on scenic tourism in the Marlborough Sounds and then Fiordland, at the southernmost end of the country.

The *Mikhail Lermontov*, with 408 passengers mainly from Australia and a predominantly Russian crew of 330, was on the second, and final, leg of her tour of the New Zealand coast, a tour widely advertised as "the cruise of a lifetime".

She had left Sydney 10 days earlier and had visited North Island ports along the East Coast before arriving in Wellington harbour the previous night. Ahead lay the part of the voyage with the most spectacular scenery. Around 3pm that same day the ship was due to leave Picton. This time she would head up the beautiful Queen Charlotte Sound to Cook Strait. A two-day run down the South Island's West Coast would end with a tour of Milford Sound in Fiordland before the liner headed back across the Tasman Sea, and home.

One of five sister-ships built for the Soviet Government's Baltic Shipping Company by Mathias Thesen Werft of Germany, she had been launched in 1972 and named, like the others, after a Russian literary giant. The *Mikhail Lermontov*, 155 metres long and 23.6 metres wide, had a laden draft of just over eight metres. She was currently under charter to CTC Cruises, an English company with offices in Australia and New Zealand.

She'd been specifically designed for the cruise market, and attention had been given to every detail of passenger comfort. A recent extensive refit had cost around NZ 36 million dollars. Altogether, she offered all the comfort and convenience of a small town at sea.

High above the water was the bridge deck with its bar with spectacular views. The sun deck and boat deck provided ample space for relaxation and sightseeing. Below these the lounge deck held a swimming pool at the stern, and amenities such as two hairdressers' salons, shops, a comprehensive library, and a movie theatre. There new movies were shown, favourites such as Beverly Hills Cops, Warning Signs, The Never-ending Story, D.A.R.R.Y.L., Goonies, Silverton and Gremlins.

Below the lounge deck was the promenade deck with palm-lined walkways running the entire length of both sides of the ship. It offered a gymnasium, massage rooms and a sauna. The next deck down held the Leningrad Restaurant with seating for about 200 people, together with a modern galley and a hospital. With the restaurant were two more decks of accommodation cabins, each with its own bathroom, and a fully equipped laundry.

Although the hull had been specially strengthened to withstand impact with ice floes, the *Mikhail Lermontov* and her permanent crew had rarely seen a winter.

During the northern hemisphere summer she operated out of Leningrad, visiting northern tourist destinations. For these cruises her hull was painted black – black to help keep the ship warmer in the Norwegian fjords. Each year she moved to Sydney before the northern winter set in. Now painted a gleaming white, from Sydney she cruised the South Pacific.

Few of the passengers on any cruise would have given a thought to their ship's communist masters. Nor would they have wondered if there was an agent of the feared secret police, the KGB, aboard. The USSR's President Gorbachev and the whole apparatus of communism were for the politicians to deal with. What the *Mikhail Lermontov* had to offer seemed a world away from politics. For the passengers, this southern summer, it was indeed as the tour brochures claimed, "the cruise of a lifetime".

In overall command of this floating luxury hotel with its permanent summer was Captain Vladislav Vorobyov. He had taken over the ship while the usual master, Captain Aram Organov, was on long-term leave.

The stocky 47-year-old Muscovite had gone to sea as an 18-year-old in 1956, and, after two years' service as a seaman, had enrolled in the Leningrad Higher Marine School. After five years he graduated and joined the Baltic Shipping Company as fourth mate. By 1979 he had proved himself a capable and reliable mariner, and was appointed staff captain of the *Alexander Pushkin*, one of the *Mikhail Lermontov's* sister ships. Once before he had commanded the *Mikhail Lermontov*, for four months in 1983, but had then returned to cargo ships until October 1985.

Now Captain Vorobyov was anxious as his ship approached the entrance to Tory Channel in the half-light of early morning. He was obeying orders to take this approach to Picton, and he had a pilot, but the approach seemed full of risks for such a large ship.

The charts clearly showed a narrow opening in the forbidding cliffs of the South Island. Lights and other navigational aids also showed they were exactly on course, but heading a large ship straight at a rocky shore – into what appeared to be nothing more than a small bay – was alien to both his training and instincts.

The Moscow captain had been in risky situations before, but here he was responsible for a total of 738 passengers and crew. And now a quiet-spoken New Zealand pilot was going to take his ship through a very narrow passage in the cliffs.

This pilot, Captain Don Jamison, was Picton harbourmaster.

He had flown from Picton to Wellington the day before with assistant harbourmaster Captain Gary Neill, to join the *Mikhail Lermontov* just before midnight. He had assumed pilotage of the ship from the Wellington pilot as they neared the South Island around 6.30am that day. Captain Vorobyov had decided they would cruise about in Cook Strait until full daylight before entering the narrow entrance to Tory Channel.

The ship's charterers had arranged for a photographer in a helicopter to take promotional photographs of the ship entering the Sounds, and there wouldn't be enough light for this until 7am. The captain knew the channel was frequently used each day by the Cook Strait ferries running between Picton and Wellington, but he also knew that most other large ships like his used the wider Northern Entrance on the western side of Arapawa Island.

Captain Vorobyov checked the charts again and saw deep water and a well-marked entrance, but he still peered anxiously through the gloom of dawn at the sea breaking on rocks. The radar also showed the entrance. He spoke in Russian to his navigator who had also checked the charts several times. The Russian navigator, too, had misgivings but said nothing in the presence of his captain. Captain Vorobyov, switching to English, then asked the pilot if he was quite sure he could get the ship through the gap. He noted the quiet confidence of the answer. There was no danger. They would soon be in the calm waters of the Tory Channel, the pilot said.

It took the Russian skipper a good deal of self-control not to question this judgment, and he felt considerable relief when they passed safely through the entrance to Tory Channel. The rocks on both sides of the ship seemed almost close enough to touch, but his tension eased as the ship swung to port and headed southwards towards Picton.

Once inside Tory Channel, the pilot pointed out the disused whaling station near the entrance. The local whaling industry had ceased some 22 years before, ironically only a few years after a large Russian whaling fleet had started working the southern ocean between New Zealand and the ice cap. The fleet had taken a huge toll of the South Pacific whale populations, and the local industry had folded after some 150 years of operations. The Perano whaling station in Tory Channel had been one of the oldest in the country, and was being restored as a historic monument to the area's pioneering past.

Cottages and cabins of the few inhabitants of this part of the Marlborough Sounds nestled in the early morning light under the steep-sided enclosing hills. A few hours previously the ship had been in Wellington harbour where the surrounding hills had been ablaze with the lights of the country's capital city, but here they could have been in the remote fjords of Norway.

Captain Vorobyov watched with quiet approval as the pilot at last guided the ship out from the narrow channel into the wider Queen Charlotte Sound. His orders to the helmsman were clear and precise. It was obvious this man was not only familiar with the area but was a very confident seaman.

Finally the helicopter with its intrusive noise departed, having acted at least as a wake-up call to passengers, and the nerve-wracking part of the morning was almost over.

In the port the Russian master watched Captain Jamison berth the big ship with the ease of an expert. He used the power of the two Sulzer diesel engines carefully and with gentle restraint. There were no tugs in Picton, but they were not needed. The pilot certainly knew what he was about. He had the ship snugly alongside Waitohi wharf quickly and quietly in the light rain, Vorobyov noted. He remembered too, that Captain Jamison had piloted the *Mikhail Lermontov's* sister ship, the *Alexander Pushkin*, on this same route the year before.

In spite of having got up extra early, Captain Vorobyov still had a seemingly endless number of decisions to make, orders to give and problems to solve before he was able to snatch a few hours' relaxation.

A ship at sea is the last truly autocratic community in the world and the captain is responsible for everyone and everything, even when he is asleep. His decisions are final, and he cannot afford to be wrong. Vorobyov knew he had a heavy responsibility, but it was one that he had worked at mastering ever since he had studied as a boy to go to sea. It hadn't been easy achieving command of Baltic Company ships but he had a reputation for being competent and trustworthy. The *Mikhail Lermontov* wasn't his usual ship but he had become thoroughly familiar with her officers, crew and routines.

Now it was another tiring day and soon he'd have visitors to entertain. At sea he followed the tradition of passenger ship captains and joined passengers at the captain's table for lunch or dinner when he could. In port, particularly a small port where the arrival of a tourist ship was something of an occasion, he was obliged to play genial host to important local people.

This seaport town of Picton had seen good times and bad over its century and a half of existence. Whalers and sealers had come and gone. An abattoir and freezing works had provided seasonal work for local people, but the works now lay idle and derelict on the western side of the harbour.

As a reminder of the past, the last of the wooden sailing scows to work on the coast had been put on blocks on the opposite shore, near the Queen Charlotte Yacht Club. Until the mid-1960s the black-hulled scow *Echo* had sailed between Wellington and Picton, and further down the east coast to the mouth of the Wairau River, then on up-river into Blenheim, the province's principal town. Shallow-drafted scows with their huge retractable centreboards, unique to the New Zealand coast, had been the lifeline of many early coastal settlements.

But the 1960s had signalled an end to the small cargo boats when a new terminal for the roll on, roll off, rail ferry service came into operation at Picton in 1962. Now ferries could carry rail and road freight, and nearly a million passengers a year, on a journey which took almost three and a half hours across the often turbulent Cook Strait.

Businesses enjoyed a boom each summer holidays when people streamed into Picton and the Sounds, some holidaying locally, some in transit. Then, as the season turned, once again it became a sleepy little town. Most of the nearly 3000 residents were happy with the arrangement. Many had jobs with the railways or the harbour board, or worked in motels, or were involved in the growing fishing industry.

Further out in the more remote areas of the Marlborough Sounds were long-established tourist lodges which used Picton as a service centre. Their smart boats and launches bobbed at moorings among a variety of other small craft on the waterfront. Alongside Waitohi wharf, larger fishing boats berthed.

The *Mikhail Lermontov* crew had already begun preparing for the day in Picton and the Sounds. Those on the night watch had gone to bed and the catering staff were getting ready for the visit of local dignitaries later that morning. Many of the passengers would be going ashore to lunch in Marlborough's vineyards during the course of sightseeing coach tours, or in Picton itself. But comfort and entertainment must still be ensured for those who elected to remain on board, and the crew had slipped into their well-oiled routine.

Wellington artist and writer Hilda Walker, the much travelled widow of a diplomat, kept diaries and a sketchbook of her voyaging, including aboard the *Mikhail Lermontov*. For the next voyage she was engaged to rejoin the ship as an art teacher for those who wanted to try their hand or become more proficient, although she wasn't aboard on this particular trip. "The whole ship is comfortable and so well organised and run," she had written to a friend. "The meals are marvellous, the cabins en suite and everything so immaculately clean it would be hard to find anything as good. It is a happy, healthy ship with no complaints whatever – amazing!"

A number of the *Mikhail Lermontov's* current passengers were also keeping diaries. Some had described the meals in detail – such as a typical luncheon menu from the newsletter given to each passenger each day, and the special event dinners, common to all cruise ships, like the Pirates' Dinner with Long John Silver's assorted pastries. To the women in particular, for many of whom the definition of "holiday" was that they didn't have to cook, this was paradise.

There were the ongoing concerts, classical and folk, with Russian and Hungarian dances. All the staff and crew, from singers and dancers to waiters and waitresses, were trained to a high standard of perfection and worked together to make the voyage a success, as more than one passenger commented.

But that wasn't all. Every moment of the day and well into the night aboard the *Mikhail Lermontov* there seemed to be something on offer. A typical day at sea went something like this:

Wake late, shower in one's en-suite bathroom, breakfast with waiter service, take the lift up one level, or, for the more energetic, climb the stairs, stroll around the promenade deck, take a few photos for the folk back home.

Sit in one of the bars writing postcards, attend a craft class. Leisurely lunch, followed by a nap. Late afternoon swim. Go to the movies, change for dinner – although serious dressing up was slightly frowned upon, on this egalitarian cruise. Dine, discussing racehorses, art and politics with one's table companions, as seen on movies featuring cruise ships.

Attend a show featuring Rita the Eta Eater of the popular Australian TV commercials – Bunny Gibson, the actress – and Horrie Dargie, the harmonica virtuoso, plus a line of real chorus girls, in the Bolshoi Lounge.

Gamble in the nightclub. Stroll round the promenade deck. Retire to one's cabin about 1am.

People who were usually busy took the opportunity to do nothing, really the greatest luxury of all. Those who lived in rural areas, where going to a gym wasn't feasible, specially revelled in the choice of sports and crafts.

As well as the active options of swimming or playing squash or deck tennis, there were the more sedate possibilities of taking a leatherwork class or making fabric flowers.

A stream of varied activities catered for the passengers, and when the ship was in port there were more choices still, from shopping and wining and dining to learning something about the history and special features of the area.

Every member of the crew had a job to do to keep things

this way, and they were encouraged to behave as if they, too, were having a wonderful time. Most of them were.

It was a pleasant ship to work in. This day, 16 February, as everyone knew, would be a little different, because it was a going-ashore day. But late afternoon would see the cruise ship back on her busy schedule.

On shore people woke to find the great white ship in port. Some had been up extra early because they themselves were to embark in Picton, to join the cruise ship for the final leg of her tour. They expected it would be a voyage they would never forget, and were anxious to get their first look at what was to be their floating home.

Others, beginning to go about their business in the light rain in the town, were also conscious of the ship's presence. Her public address system carried announcements clearly over the still waters of the quiet harbour. People listening tried to imagine the romantic, luxurious life of those on board.

A member of the long-established whaling family, Marie Perano, was out walking her dog, Joby. From across the water she heard the call for breakfast in this jewel-like ship, and paused in the rain, gazing over the harbour. Oh to be one of those lucky people, enjoying such luxury!

It would never be for her, she knew that. After a minute she called to the dog and moved on.

Those on the *Mikhail Lermontov* could look across the waterfront to an attractive children's playground among mature phoenix palms, backed by an imposing white archway, a war memorial inscribed 'To the Glorious Dead'. Next to it was Picton's whaling museum, always a target for visitors.

Hotels and shops facing the waterfront still had the picturesque facades and verandahs popular earlier in the century. Set back from the business areas, the wooden weatherboard houses with their predominantly red or green corrugated iron roofs, salt-tolerant flowers and trees and tidy lawns maintained the peaceful atmosphere.

In spite of the efforts of a few enthusiasts who wanted Picton to become a bustling tourist attraction, the town, tucked snugly under the surrounding hills, had never lost its quaint rustic appearance. The cruise ship passengers found it inviting, and prepared for the day ashore. Buses were already waiting.

It was a Sunday, and though New Zealand towns were basically 'closed', most of Picton was open for business. It looked a charming place, with people who were likely to be friendly. In Wellington the *Mikhail Lermontov* had been just another cruise ship in town, whereas here, because Picton was so small, the impact of the visit was greater, and they would be treated as special guests.

In the event, the passengers did all the usual things. They pottered and looked and talked and explained. They bought woollen jerseys, trinkets, and bottles, even cases, of the area's famous wines. Nothing whatsoever in the peaceful countryside, or in the hospitable small town, could have prepared them for what lay ahead.

Passengers Ray and Lorna Leihn and their two grandsons had been up at 6.30am for an early breakfast and were determined to take in the sights of Marlborough in spite of the rain.

The boys – John, just eight years old, and his brother Steven, five – were full of energy and enthusiasm but weren't interested in the town or its history. It was their first big trip away from their New South Wales home and they wanted to have a ride on a catamaran and feed the tame fish they had read about. They wanted about a million other things as well, but their Nana and Pa were not going to be hurried. A bus trip was first on the list of things to do that day, Lorna said, and they would see about other things later.

The Leihns took one of the special buses bound inland for Blenheim, to see the sights and then return via the scenic route along Queen Charlotte Drive. By mid-morning the boys said they were starving. When the bus stopped at a tea shop at the small seaside town of Havelock the boys wolfed scones with cream and jam as if they hadn't been fed for a week. Their grandmother called a halt. There was still some way to go before they got back to the port and she knew about little boys with tummy aches. That would mean going straight back to the ship, and she wanted to see the shops.

In Picton the buses continued to line up to take people sightseeing, or around the local wineries a few kilometres inland. The whole place had a carnival air in spite of the persistent rain. But after their big morning tea and the trip over winding roads, the Leihn family was glad to be back.

First came a quick look at the shops, and then the boys finally persuaded their grandparents to take a ride on the catamaran. The *Beachcomber* was spacious and they were able to relax. The rain stopped for a while, and it was warm in spite of heavy cloud which clung to the surrounding hills.

The *Beachcomber* cruised Queen Charlotte Sound for a couple of hours, dropping off and picking up people from secluded bays and remote jetties on the way. Many of the homes and farms in the Marlborough Sounds are accessible only by boat, and the Leihns marvelled at this lifestyle. On the way they stopped at Double Cove and John and Steven helped feed the shoal of tame fish which swam expectantly around the hull.

By the time they got back to the ship the boys had finally run out of energy, at least for a few hours, and a quiet afternoon was in store. The rain resumed against the windows of their cabin. It had a soothing effect and they were soon sleeping off their adventures.

Typical of those who had an uneventful day was Geoffrey Naughton. At 39, he was one of the younger passengers, from New South Wales, and single. He went ashore, didn't find much to see or do in town, and tried to find a drink. This took a little time as it was a Sunday, and even though Picton was a port, "it sure wasn't crammed full of 24-hour sailors' bars".

Geoffrey had prior seafaring experience; as a firm believer in cruises being the only way to have a proper holiday, he had already been on four liners, and had also worked in an American research ship along the edge of the Antarctic pack ice.

In Picton, he had lunch in the Moby Dick Restaurant and headed back in the drizzle to the *Mikhail Lermontov*. There hadn't been anything to excite him.

Clare Stevenson, of Kings Cross, Sydney, stood out in any group. A natural leader, a feisty fighter for social justice and a fun-loving 'people person', she was liked and respected at all levels of society. The fact that she was 82 was just that – a fact. She had no intention of letting age restrict her many public activities, or stop her enjoying life. Hence this cruise.

The Russian women crew members had quickly become very fond of her. One of them, off-duty, persuaded her to go ashore and look around, although the rain had initially made her decide to stay aboard.

What the crew and nearly all of the passengers didn't realise was that Clare Stevenson, so natural and easy to talk with, was highly respected and appreciated for her services to the community, particularly for her work to improve life for the aged, war veterans, and those who stayed at home to care for others. As long ago as 1960 she had been honoured for this work with an MBE in the Queen's Birthday Honours List, and this cruise was one of the few breaks she had taken from her community work.

Some of the elderly passengers, particularly those from New South Wales, did know about her work on the NSW Council on the Ageing, specially its off-shoot, the Carers' Association of New South Wales, which Clare had established and chaired. Just three months previously she had succeeded in having the word 'carer' embodied in legislation when the Carers Pension was introduced. This at once brought financial relief to thousands, mostly women, who had given up their own jobs to look after frail or disabled relatives or friends in private dwellings.

Two years on from this cruise of the *Mikhail Lermontov*, Clare Stevenson was to receive more honours: the City of Sydney's Community Award for her volunteer work, and a place in the list of 200 names selected by the Australian Bicentennial Authority for honouring as unsung heroes and heroines.

The Russian women crew had no inkling of this

background. Like so many others, they simply responded to Clare as a person, 'a beaut Australian'. They knew they weren't supposed to socialise with the passengers, but that wasn't something you thought of when you with with Clare Stevenson. They had been teaching her to count in Russian. Her early attempts to master the difficult words had given everyone a lot of fun, but she stuck to the task with impressive determination. That night she and many others would have reason to be thankful for her perseverance with her lessons.

But now, in the morning rain, she and the off-duty stewardess walked from the cruise ship across by the seafront gardens into Picton. They chatted and admired handcrafts in the gift shops until Clare began to feel cold. She was still full of energy and was enjoying the sights of the little town, but knew better than to risk getting a chill on a rainy day. In any case, the permanent, piercing pain in her legs – pain which she usually ignored – was telling her it was time to return to the trip.

Besides, there was to be more Russian folk dancing that night and the former WAAF didn't want to miss out on the sort of fun she had so enjoyed when she was young. Russian music or not, if she got half a chance she would persuade everyone to join in – age no barrier – and turn it into a good old-fashioned Aussie 'knees up'.

Mark Raymond, a 26-year-old bus depot operator from Dharruk in New South Wales, was among those who had also taken the chance for a few hours off the ship. The light rain was only a slight annoyance, and the shopping centre was quaint and interesting after the expanse and complexity of Wellington.

By noon he was beginning to feel hungry and stopped at a tea shop near the waterfront. When the rain increased, Mark decided the best place to be was back in his cabin on the ship. In any case they were due to sail before too long, and there was the evening's entertainment to look forward to.

Busloads of sightseeing passengers were returning at intervals, carrying cameras, souvenirs and bottles of wine from the vineyards. They chatted with those who'd taken different tours, and had a brief look at the town and its attractions.

Many of the elderly Australians, comparing notes back on board, decided Picton was similar to towns they knew at home. They'd enjoyed being in the quiet little shops, some with bare wooden floors, and friendly staff who were happy to chat.

There was no sign or portent of the drama which would be played out over the next 24 hours, stripping away the peaceful exterior and giving people nightmares for years. It was to be a drama which would take an innocent life, and lay bare an ulcer of petty local politics and personal vendettas within the Marlborough Harbour Board, one which would eventually cost the whole community millions of dollars.

On this quiet Sunday the well-appointed Marlborough Harbour Board building in Picton's Auckland Street looked remote and detached. The arrival of busy staff the next day would change the atmosphere, but for now all was at peace.

In the foyer the five-foot high, wooden-spoked helm of the scow *Echo* stood on a pedestal near an old-style kerosene-powered navigation light. The helm had been donated by harbour board member Tom Eckford, one of the last owners of the scow while she was working on the coast.

On the wall a set of brass-mounted marine chronometers and barometers gleamed in the subdued lighting. In a glass case a large lump of glistening black coal had been mounted, along with technical details of its qualities as steamship fuel. The coal had come from an exploratory mine near Shakespeare Bay, just around the headland from Picton.

The board's coat of arms and deeply varnished fittings also proclaimed that this was the workplace of seafarers and master mariners.

Most elected harbour board members had some association with the sea or shipping. They proudly wore their dark wine-coloured ties and blazers, with impressive pocket emblems, to meetings of the board. Then the well-stocked bar next to the boardroom, with its deep leather seats and wall photographs of the harbour and significant ships, completed a picture of calm assurance and superiority over trifling affairs.

Behind this bland and well-ordered exterior, however, a running sore had been festering for almost a decade. The seat of the problem was in the Marlborough Harbour Board itself, an elected local authority which served the wider community, and which was trying to keep the lid on a bitter internal dispute.

The board had a comfortable income of around $5 million a year, a substantial amount in the local economy of the day, in berthage fees paid by New Zealand Rail for the Cook Strait ferries. In addition there was less regular revenue from other shipping. But the board was seriously and bitterly divided over senior staff appointments.

One senior officer in the long-running conflict, the board's previous general manager, Mike Goulden, had been dismissed by the board two years earlier, and was currently involved in a bitter legal battle with them, over his dismissal.

This Sunday another of those senior officers, harbourmaster and pilot Captain Don Jamison, was back in his office. In the midst of the ongoing legal warfare the business of the harbour board still had to be managed, but it had become a very different operation from that of bygone years.

Mike Goulden had established a new staff structure which needed a full-time manager, and now Don Jamison found himself doing three jobs. For more than a year he had been acting general manager as well as harbourmaster and pilot. On top of all this he was actively involved in the board's defence against Mike Goulden's dismissal appeal, which was still before the court.

In fact Don Jamison had still been in the witness box on the previous Friday, a gruelling experience, but the case had been adjourned for three weeks, an arrangement enabling him to go off on the *Mikhail Lermontov*. He was also in the middle of training new harbour pilot Captain Gary Neill, who had recently joined the board's staff. It was a huge workload.

Don Jamison was making final arrangements for a relief pilot to take his place while he was away. He had been working up to 80 hours a week for the past year, and was due to take a week's leave, beginning as soon as he had fulfilled his contract to pilot the *Mikhail Lermontov*. More details of paperwork had to be finalised and then he could put the harbour board and all its troubles behind him for a few days.

Later that afternoon he would pilot the ship out of Queen Charlotte Sound, as he had on previous occasions piloted vessels of similar size, including the sister ship *Alexander Pushkin*. On the way out he would give another of his commentaries over the ship's public address system. It was something he enjoyed doing, having the ship listen to him while he described the scenic and historic features of the area, matters which were so familiar to him.

When the ship reached the outer limit of the Marlborough Harbour Board's jurisdiction near Motuara Island, he would begin his leave from work. He'd be able to relax and be one of the pampered passengers himself as the ship travelled down the rugged West Coast. Then, two days later, he would give more commentaries when they reached Milford Sound. He would stay aboard until the ship reached Sydney, flying home when the ship's tour ended there.

Fine weather was forecast. It was just the time away from stress and work that he needed.

CHAPTER TWO

The Decision

BY MID-MORNING a string of dignitaries and other visitors had begun arriving and boarding the cruise ship. Vladislav Vorobyov stopped being captain and assumed the role of ambassador. It was a role he could enjoy for an hour or two at a time, but after that it began to weigh on him.

To the Russians these New Zealanders were strange people. Some dressed as if for a casual holiday and others were confined in hot formal suits in New Zealand's summer. Although many appeared affluent by the way they dressed, they were not accustomed to paying tourist prices. One passenger, who was leaving the ship at Picton, his home town, was heard to complain loudly at the cost of a bottle of cordial he had bought on board for his wife.

Few spoke anything but English, but their accent was harder to understand than American English. They were particularly affable and welcoming to strangers, and they seemed to laugh at almost nothing. The visitors could drink as much beer as Captain Vorobyov would give them but they didn't know how to deal with vodka. He had watched with silent amusement as some of the men threw down small glasses of the fiery drink in what they assumed was the proper Russian manner, only to lose their breath and very soon their tongues. The women were more discreet with alcohol and seemed genuinely interested in Russian customs. He chatted in his best English and kept them amused with tales of shipboard life.

The captain restricted his own drinking to non-alcoholic cordials. When he accepted the command, he had resolved not to drink alcohol on board the ship. Even ashore he was an expert at making a drink last so long that it became tepid and almost undrinkable. He had also learned to eat lightly before a long night shift on the bridge. Keeping awake on night duty was an essential skill. Now he had to see the day through, as well as the evening's entertainment, besides taking over on the bridge when the ship reached western Cook Strait later that day.

At noon Captain Jamison closed his office and walked down the wet street to Waitohi wharf where he and harbour board chairman Bruno Dalliessi were to make a presentation to the captain of the *Mikhail Lermontov*.

Captain Jamison stayed for a quick lunch with the ship's agent and local friends. While the ship's catering staff had done their usual excellent job with elegantly presented finger-food for casual visitors, a more formal lunch for those connected with the harbour board received more than the usual compliments.

Jamison had become accustomed to rushed lunches and long hours of work, but it would be good to relax and have time for himself. He was looking forward to getting away from Picton. Back in his office he completed arrangements so he could return to the cruise ship just in time to take her out.

Vladislav Vorobyov was also glad when the entertaining was over. He'd enjoyed the visitors' company and friendliness, but now he was impatient to get underway when the last of the sightseers, and the new passengers from Picton, had embarked.

From shore many eyes watched the *Mikhail Lermontov* pull slowly out from the wharf. Only the weather had marred her visit, but she and other cruise ships would be back, and Picton and the whole province would welcome them.

On board the ship the passengers were settling back into their roles at sea. Before they headed up Queen Charlotte Sound to Cook Strait, Captain Jamison announced over the public address system, he wanted to give them a quick look at Shakespeare Bay, just around the western headland from the harbour. There the hulk of the wooden sailing ship *Edwin Fox* lay abandoned near the shore, waiting for public interest, and financial support, to bring her round to Picton for restoration.

The historic *Edwin Fox*, he explained over the ship's public address system, was an East Indiaman built in Calcutta in 1853. It had been used to take troops to the Crimean War, and had transported convicts to Australia and immigrants to New Zealand. The old ship had even seen the beginning of the frozen meat trade to Britain – all this before ending its days as a coal hulk alongside the Picton freezing works. When the works had closed in 1964 the hulk had been hauled out of sight to Shakespeare Bay, and left to rot. Now, as the *Mikhail Lermontov* steamed slowly in the picturesque little bay, the *Edwin Fox* could be seen lying forlornly in the shallows, a reminder, perhaps, of how even a proud vessel has an uncertain future.

The cruise ship was moving slowly ahead but she seemed to be having trouble turning out of Shakespeare Bay. Captain Jamison's order to the helmsman, to turn the ship to starboard, did not appear to be having the effect he wanted, although obviously it had been fully understood.

Don Jamison signalled to the engine room to stop the starboard engine and put it in reverse, and ordered the bow thruster to be activated to starboard. The ship was still not responding fast enough. The starboard engine was put full astern. The *Mikhail Lermontov* seemed to be heading straight for the rocky beach.

Vladislav Vorobyov and his senior officers on the bridge were becoming distinctly anxious. Don Jamison stepped out on to the wing of the bridge to get a closer look before deciding what next to do. He was expert at manoeuvring big ships in confined spaces, but the bow thruster did not seem to be operating.

As he was about to return to the bridge to give further instructions, he lost his footing on the wet grating. He fell heavily on his back, losing his glasses and the keys from his pocket. Russian officers hurried to help him to his feet, and he prepared to return to the task of turning the ship away from the beach.

But the moment the pilot had fallen to the deck, Captain Vorobyov had stepped in, taken control of the situation, and ordered both engines to be put full astern.

The ship stopped at right angles to the beach, about 30 metres from the rocks. This was far, far too close for the comfort of an ocean-going master mariner. He liked several kilometres between his ship and the nearest land.

An investigation by the assistant harbourmaster, Captain Neill, again on board to watch and learn, revealed that the bow thruster motor had been turned off. A bow thruster, which consumes a lot of power, is normally turned off after a ship has cleared its berth.

No-one had checked with the pilot to see if he wanted this done, and he had assumed the bow thruster motors were still running. They were restored to operation, and used to get the ship out of the confines of the bay.

The passengers, meanwhile, were impressed by the close view they were getting. Only a few knew there had been any kind of alarming incident.

Captain Vorobyov spoke to the deck officer in Russian, and warned him against letting the pilot take the ship in too close to the shore again. He then spoke to Captain Jamison in clear English. He asked him to keep the ship further offshore, and to set a course up Queen Charlotte Sound to the open waters of Cook Strait.

There was some concern in case Don Jamison had hurt himself when he fell so heavily. He assured those around him, however, that he was perfectly all right. What he didn't tell them was how tired he was. The lengthy legal dispute between the harbour board and its former general manager had added a huge mental burden to his already significant workload.

As they left Shakespeare Bay, Vorobyov agreed to let the pilot take the ship down the north-western side of Queen Charlotte Sound after he'd said the misty rain would obscure the scenery for the passengers if they took the usual course down the centre of the Sound.

Captain Vorobyov was wet, and he too was tired. He'd been caught in the rain several times during the day while meeting and farewelling visitors, and hadn't had time to change. His damp uniform was uncomfortable and he was feeling the chill of the overcast afternoon. It had been a long, eventful day after too little sleep the night before, and he was looking forward to being in dry clothes well before the formal dinner he had to host later that evening.

Afterwards there would be music and Russian dancing. He intended to slip away from this, but first he'd be expected to sit at the head of the captain's table.

Now from the bridge of the *Mikhail Lermontov* he looked out on the drab afternoon as the 20,000-tonne Soviet liner nosed gently up Queen Charlotte Sound. A few small yachts dotted the slightly ruffled water in Picton harbour. It was just after 3pm, and the yachts' brightly coloured sails stood out against the rain-shrouded hills behind. The old-world charm of the still-visible seaside town would make a delightful picture for everyone to remember.

Further out were larger yachts with white and yellow sails, and powerboats whose wakes foamed across the dark green of the deeper sea. The steep hills of the Sound loomed large and damp and ancient in the low cloud which clung to the farther peaks.

Vladislav Vorobyov's first impression of the South Island had been of clean open spaces, and of people who were friendly and generous. To this he'd added their love of boating. He stood for another moment watching while the helmsman responded to the directions of Captain Jamison, relayed through the interpreting deck officer.

They headed towards Allports Island, the bush-covered sentinel at the combined mouths of four bays on both shores of the Sound. Commercial ships normally passed the island on the south-east side, but Captain Jamison took the ship between the island and the nor'west shore so the passengers could have another close-up view.

After passing Allports Island the ship headed closely past Golden Point which juts into the Sound from the nor'western shore. Captain Vorobyov once more became concerned.

He distinctly did not like the way the pilot took the ship so close to Golden Point. Why was he doing this? It was an alarming risk. In spite of not liking to repeat himself, and perhaps risk offending the pilot, he did speak to him again about the need to keep further offshore.

Altogether there was no way Captain Vorobyov could enjoy the pilot's willingness to hug the shoreline, no matter how much some passengers were enjoying the chance to take photographs. This was a big ocean liner, and the ultimate responsibility was the captain's.

By 3.20pm his physical discomfort began to out-weigh his continuing concern about the earlier shore-hugging. He needed a shower and dry clothes, and the best opportunity would come soon. The ship was still under the direction of the pilot, who was giving one of his detailed commentaries on the features around them. Vorobyov made a quick check of the ship's position and duty rosters, and decided he should stay on the bridge until the change of watch at 4pm, when his senior navigator, Sergey Stepanishchev, and the second mate, Sergey Gusev, came on duty.

At 4pm Anatoliy Burin relieved the helmsman, and the previous watch went off duty. With his senior navigation officer and second mate now on the bridge with the pilot, the captain felt confident he could go below. But he remained on the bridge until after the assistant harbourmaster, Gary Neill, had disembarked on to the pilot launch near Luke Rock, and the ship was then brought up to 15 knots.

The weather was closing in but there were no other ships in the area. They had a straight run to the open waters of Cook Strait, this time not through the narrow confines of Tory Channel, but out the hospitably wide Northern Entrance of Queen Charlotte Sound. Here they would turn westwards past the Cape Jackson lighthouse and out around narrow Farewell Spit before running down the West Coast.

The pilot was giving quiet commands to helmsman Burin, and continuing to use the public address system to entertain the passengers with details of the historic area.

Captain Vorobyov was interested in seeing Ship Cove, then about 40 minutes away, where Captain James Cook had first landed in 1770. He knew the Russian Navy had also been there 50 years later, during the height of Russian global explorations.

Captain Fabian Gottlieb Von Bellingshausen, on the 28-gun, 900-ton sloop *Vostok*, together with Captain Larzarev on the similar ship *Mirnyy*, had headed an Antarctic expedition from 1819 to 1821. In May 1820 a heavy storm had caught both ships in mid-Tasman a few days out from the British colony in New South Wales. After 18 days of rough weather the Russians had decided to shelter in Queen Charlotte Sound, which had been named by Captain Cook the year after Bellingshausen had been born. Bellingshausen had been an admiring student of the British explorer's work and had wanted to see for himself the area Captain Cook had charted.

The two Russian ships sailed into Ship Cove on May 27 1820, and were met by several canoe-loads of Maori who made them welcome. The Russians spent a fascinated and harmonious week with their Rangitane and Ngati Kuia hosts, who apparently roamed freely through the ships, helping out with hoisting sails as some refitting was done, singing loudly as they did so.

In return the Russians were allowed to inspect the pa at Cannibal Cove, named years earlier by Cook. Detailed notes taken by the observant Russians record a robust, healthy population who were keen to barter their tools, clothes and weapons for the blankets, nails and axes of their visitors.

The chief's daughter received a mirror, "in order that she might convince herself that she surpassed all other women in beauty", Bellingshausen recorded. More practically, seeds of turnips, carrots, pumpkins, large beans and peas were given, with instructions about planting them. Potatoes were already there, having been brought by Cook, but were not yet abundant.

Sketches of the Maori people and notes of their songs and language, made by expedition artists, still exist in Russian museums. Many artefacts were also collected and carefully catalogued before the Russians left the area. They included 'hurlbats' of greenstone, presumably mere.

As it turned out, they had made their accurate description of the Rangitane and Ngati Kuia people and their culture just before it was all but wiped out in the devastating raids of musket-armed North Island tribes, led by the notorious war chief Te Rauparaha, which began about 1826.

Only a mere six years later there were few survivors, and much of the oral history and original Maori culture of the Sounds area was lost for ever.

Captain Vorobyov thought it would be good for everyone to see this historic area and hear what the pilot had to say about it, so he agreed to let Captain Jamison take the *Mikhail Lermontov* into Ship Cove before heading out to sea. They looked at the charts of Queen Charlotte Sound together and decided on the course the ship would take.

Although he had been seriously disturbed by the Shakespeare Bay and Golden Point incidents, after this latest talk Captain Vorobyov felt sure the pilot would heed his instruction to keep the ship further off the shore. He had accepted the report from his officers that the bow thruster motor had been turned off. The near-mishap hadn't altogether been the fault of the pilot. And the Golden Point incident might also not have been as serious as it had seemed, because the pilot certainly appeared to be thoroughly familiar with the Sounds. He was the man with the local knowledge, and he exuded confidence.

Captain Vorobyov would normally have stayed on the bridge until the ship was completely out of enclosed waters but now, he decided, it was all right to go below. Speaking quietly to chief navigator Stepanishchev, he told him he would be in his cabin, and to call him when they reached Ship Cove.

Anticipating his captain's requirements, his steward had laid out a fresh uniform and prepared the usual refreshment tray in his cabin, which was on the starboard side of the ship, so he couldn't see Ship Cove and the western shore. Captain Vorobyov was cold. He had a hot shower, then sat and worked at his desk. He was behind with his routine paper work and was anxious to clear some of it while he had the chance.

While he worked, his mind wandered over the events of

the day. He thought he had detected tension between Jamison and some members of the harbour board. Perhaps it had been only his imagination although, on closer study, the pilot appeared drawn and rather tired. They were both about the same age so perhaps the lack of sleep the night before and socialising during the day had also affected the pilot. The Shakespeare Bay and Golden Point incidents had certainly given him doubts about the man's competence, but surely he could now dismiss such thoughts.

His reverie was interrupted by the telephone on his desk. "Captain, we are nearing Ship Cove, sir."

"Thank you," he replied. Hanging up, he reflected on the administrative details he still had to work through. If he went up on deck, he'd get no more work done. No, the view of this historic place could wait until another time. He would carry on at his desk for a while. He felt the ship turn into Ship Cove, and heard the pilot using the public address system to explain about Captain Cook's arrival 200 years ago.

This was of interest to many of the Australian passengers, as Captain Cook also had an important place in their history.

Lorna Leihn was writing down as much of Captain Jamison's commentary as she could. She would be able to explain it all to the boys later. She wanted to take them out on deck to show them the landing place, but it was wet and cold and the boys were quiet after their busy day. Little Steven in fact was fast asleep, and John was colouring in a picture they had picked up earlier, of a local church.

The boys had enjoyed the North Island part of the tour, particularly a visit to Rotorua after the ship berthed at Tauranga. There they had been to a model Maori village where traditional hangi-cooked food had been served for lunch. Eating his food "cooked in a hole in the ground" had been a bit too much for Ray, but the boys had enjoyed it.

Later they'd been entertained by a Maori concert party, and John, happy to show off, had accepted an invitation to join the Maori girls dancing on stage, to everyone's delight.

Only four more days to go, Lorna Leihn thought, and they'd

be back home again – but what memories they would have. The boys were the youngest passengers on board and everybody had spoiled them. She hoped they would remember most of their adventures, and, if they didn't, her note-taking would help her to remind them about it.

Captain Vorobyov had been pleased to hear reports from his chief steward about how interested some of the passengers had been in the informative talks the pilot had given earlier. That counterbalanced his niggling concern about the pilot's willingness to take the ship close inshore. Still, the Sounds were very deep and the pilot was surely skilled at such manoeuvres. Certainly he would speak to him again about the matter before they got to Milford Sound, where they were scheduled to take a sightseeing tour of the famous deep-water Sounds before heading for Australia.

Nevertheless he didn't relax completely until he felt the ship turn slightly as it headed out of Ship Cove. At full speed the big propellers bit into the water at 95 revolutions a minute, slowly building the ship's speed to 15 knots again. The gyro repeater compass in the captain's room showed they were heading for the open waters of Cook Strait. Soon they would reach the pilotage limit of the Marlborough Sounds, and his ship would be under his command, even if the pilot was still on board as a passenger. Shortly beyond Motuara Island they would pass Cape Jackson, with the Cape Jackson lighthouse perched on a pinnacle of jagged rock, and then turn westwards around Walker Rock to the open sea, and Farewell Spit.

Robert and Enid Diffin were among the few passengers out on the port side upper deck, watching the scenery drift by, and listening to the pilot's commentary on the public address system. The rain added a mysterious and desolate air to the scene, which appeared almost devoid of human structures apart from an occasional, easily-overlooked, small jetty. They could imagine they were seeing what Captain Cook had seen.

About 20 minutes after leaving Ship Cove, the Diffins observed how near the ship was to the beach. It seemed to be speeding past just out of reach. "By jove, that was close," Robert remarked to his wife as the ship passed so near to the shore that he could see every detail of the rocky shoreline. They watched as the ship's wake pounded along the shore, keeping up not far astern of the speeding vessel.

From his cabin on the starboard side of the ship, Captain Vorobyov was unable to see how close they now were to shore. He looked out his cabin porthole and saw they were passing Motuara Island. Although he should now have gone to the bridge to relieve the pilot, or have called the bridge to instruct his senior navigator to take over, because they were nearing the harbour pilotage limits, he decided to leave Captain Jamison on the bridge until they were in the open waters of Cook Strait. It would be only a few minutes more. He would relieve the pilot when they cleared Cape Jackson, he thought. And a few more minutes would see his paper work up to date. Shortly afterwards he felt the ship swing her bows to port and begin to steady on her new course. Just a few minutes more and he would go to the bridge.

Joan Dillon had spent an interesting day in Picton but was one of many now feeling weary. She was looking forward to the evening's entertainment and was enjoying a relaxing shower before getting changed. In their double cabin her daughter, Gail Cottle, was resting on her bed. Mrs Dillon's second husband had died six months previously, and Gail had persuaded the 56-year-old widow to take a trip on the cruise ship to help her recover from her grief.
    The two women had enjoyed the visits to North Island ports and were looking forward to more South Island scenery. It was a pity the rain had almost spoiled their view of the Marlborough Sounds and they were hoping for clear weather when they reached the bottom of the South Island where the scenery was reputed to be even more spectacular.

Up on the ship's bridge, chief navigator Sergey Stepanishchev was anxious. He moved to the engine telegraph on the bridge in case he needed to manoeuvre the *Mikhail Lermontov* quickly. He had hoped the master would be back on the bridge by now to take over from the pilot. They had passed the pilotage limits, and the pilot should have handed the ship over to either the master or the senior officer by now.

He had called the master when they reached Ship Cove, as ordered, but the captain had not returned to the bridge and Sergey did not like the way the pilot was hugging the coastline of Queen Charlotte Sound. His anxiety had begun before he came on duty, when the ship had stopped with her bow seemingly just metres from the stony beach near Shakespeare Bay, and he wanted the reassuring presence of the captain back on his bridge.

The officers whom Sergey Stepanishchev had relieved at 4pm had told him the pilot had almost run the ship aground when the bow thrusters didn't operate properly. Then Captain Vorobyov had ordered the pilot to keep the ship further from the shore after they passed behind Allports Island and steamed too close to Golden Point. There had also been some discussion among the Russian officers about the course out of the Marlborough Sounds. The course had been discussed, agreed on and plotted on the chart, but the pilot had insisted on taking the ship closer to the nor'western shore than the course indicated he would.

Ship Cove had looked green and dripping wet from the bridge but the navigator had been too busy logging each change of direction to take much notice of the historic landing place. The *Mikhail Lermontov* had maintained full speed and turned into the wide cove where James Cook had found safe haven for his sea-weary crew in 1769. Don Jamison had again been on the public address system, telling the passengers the fascinating story of New Zealand's discovery by the British, (who in that day and age tended to ignore the fact that sea-going Polynesians, not to mention Abel Tasman, had discovered it first), and reminding the Australian passengers of their equally historic links with Cook.

Apart from a small concrete monument, a short jetty and two tiny shed-like huts back among the trees, the cove had looked much as it might have been all those years ago. The hills surrounding the cove were thickly covered in dripping native bush, and seabirds glided forlornly along the rocky beach.

The ship had swung her bows to starboard out of the cove, and the few passengers on deck had put their cameras away and hurried back inside out of the wet. It had grown colder, and they had seen enough wet scenery for the day. Even Australians from the most dry parts of their country had found that the novelty of rain, drizzle, and more rain, had worn off.

Sergey Stepanishchev felt relieved when they emerged from Ship Cove. Now they had a short, straight run out to the open waters of Cook Strait. As if sharing his relief, the ship started to 'feel' the slight influence of sea swell and began, ever so gently, to dip her bows in the regular motion so familiar to blue water sailors. His relief was short-lived. The pilot directed the helmsman to steer the ship to port when they reached Waihi Point, and he again kept the ship close to the shore. Directly ahead Sergey could see Walker Rock to the nor'east of Cape Jackson lighthouse.

Speaking in Russian, Second Mate Sergey Gusev, able to contain his anxiety no longer, told the chief navigator he thought they were too close to the shore. Captain Jamison spoke no Russian, but the sailors knew he must have some idea from their faces and tones of voice that they were concerned, no matter how professionally they tried to behave. Twice that day they had both heard their captain warn the pilot. "You should ask the pilot why he has taken us in this close," Gusev recommended.

The chief navigator agreed. Speaking in English, he asked, "Captain, why are you taking the ship into such a dangerous place?" The pilot said he was going to give the passengers a close look at Cape Jackson. It would be their last chance to enjoy the scenery of the Sounds before they headed out to sea.

The second mate and the chief navigator looked at each other briefly. There were only a few cable lengths of the shoreline left before they were in open water, and then the pilot would go off duty and they could both relax.

The next moment the Russians were astonished to hear the pilot order, "Helm, port ten degrees."

Sergey Gusev questioned the order. "I can see a line of white water in there – what is he doing?" he asked his senior officer. There was a ring of genuine anxiety in his voice.

Sergey Stepanishchev shared his concern, asking in English, "Captain, why are you taking us in so close?"

"There is no need to worry, there is plenty of water here," came the confident reply.

The big cruise ship was turning at 15 knots through the passage between Cape Jackson and the Cape Jackson lighthouse, and the navigator could see a line of white water indicating shallows or opposing currents directly ahead. If the currents suddenly pushed her off course at this speed, this close to shore, rudders might be too slow to get the ship out of trouble. It could take several long seconds for the big ship to respond, although putting one or both engines astern could give a quicker response if they were heading for trouble.

The pilot spoke directly to the helmsman, ordering "Midships," to steady the big ship as she obeyed the rudders. And again the pilot ordered, "Port ten."

The two Russian officers were now acutely anxious. Even if, miraculously, their captain had arrived on the bridge, it was too late to countermand the order. The big ship simply did not have enough room to turn away from the passage without running aground on the lighthouse, and they were moving too fast to stop in time.

Ahead they could see, more clearly as they approached it, the line of troubled water where two powerful currents met. They both knew they had no business taking the ship through the passage.

The navigator gripped the telegraph handles. There was a cold knot in his belly. His mind raced. He should have stopped this foolishness at Waihi Point and kept the ship heading out to sea. He could have countermanded the pilot at any time after the master had left the bridge. He was the senior officer on the bridge and responsible. Now it was too late to alter course.

How he hated being on the bridge of a big ship close to a rocky shore. Ice he knew and understood – ships and ice almost belonged together in a relationship of mutual respect. Rocks were always dangerous. "When the Old Man sees the chart of where we've been there'll be hell to pay," he thought.

The line of disturbed white water parted and disappeared under her bow as the ship, still coming around under port helm, headed through the passage. In a few minutes they would be through it and the navigator would lay a course to the north of d'Urville Island and around Farewell Spit. Then, whatever else was happening, he would call the master again.

"Midships," ordered the pilot, and the helmsman centred the rudders. "Steady so," the pilot ordered, and again the helmsman steadied the swing of the bows.

Directly below the bridge, in the Bolshoi Lounge, Mark Raymond had joined other passengers for a wine-tasting hour. Most of his fellow passengers were resting in their cabins although a few were watching the last of the Marlborough Sounds through observation windows. Mark had heard the local pilot, over the public address system, telling the passengers he was signing off for the night and would resume his commentary when they reached Milford Sound in two days' time. Meanwhile Mark was due to go in to the second sitting for dinner later that evening, but he was feeling hungry, and the food presented with the wines looked good.

He'd been to Auckland on a previous cruise and had wanted to see more of New Zealand. Although he wasn't one of the wine buff set he enjoyed good wines, and the ship's caterers had bought several cases of some top Marlborough vintages. Cheeses, both local and from all over the world, also tempted him. The dancing was starting and Mark was looking forward to the flamboyant display. He settled down to enjoy the hour.

Noeline Rodger was one of 14 New Zealanders who'd joined the ship in Auckland. She had had a hip operation which hadn't been a great success so agreed with her sister-in-law, Audrey Peterson of Cambridge, when she said what they both needed was "a lovely holiday to get right away from it all". So far that was just what they had both been doing. They went out on Picton harbour in a catamaran and enjoyed a bus tour. As for souvenirs, Noeline preferred the goods in the Russian shop aboard, so bought a number of beautiful and inexpensive bowls and spoons and took them to her cabin. There she'd rested until changing into her cocktail gear for the wine tasting in the Bolshoi Lounge.

Tom Archer, from Campbelltown in New South Wales, was a 74-year-old Australian who liked nothing better than a good social evening with music and a drink or two. He, his wife Dorothy and sister-in-law Sheila Simpson were also at the wine-tasting.

Together they made up a cross-section of the happy, relaxed passengers in the Bolshoi Lounge who were watching a line of chorus girls doing the 'bird dance' before the more traditional Russian dancing got under way. It was, they agreed, shaping up to be a night to remember.

CHAPTER THREE

The Rocks

CAPTAIN VOROBYOV was ready to return to the bridge. He saw that the gyro compass repeater in his cabin had swung to 030 degrees, and knew that this was about the time Captain Jamison's pilot duties should end. He was mildly relieved. Now they must be into the open waters of Cook Strait, on course to head westwards towards Farewell Spit.

He combed his hair and straightened his tie in front of the cabin mirror and stepped out of his cabin, heading to the bridge. It was 5.37pm.

Then the deck beneath him heaved.

My god, have we hit a submerged container – or another ship?

Containers often fell from ships during heavy weather and could drift for weeks or even months before finally sinking. Some, with buoyant cargo, had been known to stay afloat for years. If they were mostly below the surface they were almost impossible to detect, even with radar.

But would a container be big enough to jolt the 20,000-tonne *Mikhail Lermontov*? The captain's mind was in turmoil as he hurtled to the bridge. There was no panic, just frantic speculation. He'd been aboard ships which had hit ice floes, but these impacts – there was another, and another, as he ran – were harsher, and unyielding. A container would have been bouncing away from them after the collision. This was not.

This object they had obviously hit – would it have penetrated the German-built hull? This had been reinforced to withstand hitting ice but it was still vulnerable, as all ship's hulls were. Later he could not recall how many shocks in total ran through the ship before he burst on to the bridge, other senior officers almost falling through the door after him.

Mark Raymond had found a comfortable seat in a corner of the Bolshoi Lounge to enjoy his second glass of red wine when a sudden severe jolt, accompanied by a harsh scraping sound, almost threw him from his chair.

Stewards had carefully set out glasses of wine on the buffet table. They went flying. Several people who were standing in groups lurched, and either fell or almost lost their footing.

Through the window Mark could see a lighthouse. To him and to most non-sailors, a lighthouse was the very symbol of disasters, remembered from childhood storybooks as associated with wrecks and wreckers.

Whatever was happening? The buzz of conversation around him had come to a sudden shocked halt. Everyone in the lounge asked themselves the same silent question.

Noeline Rodger had been sipping white wine and appreciatively watching the Russian dancing. "I was thinking 'This is the life. Aren't I lucky to be here. Everything is so beautiful and so lovely' when the ship gave a terrific lurch. It was a real 'graunch', as though it had hit a wharf."

Glasses flew off tables but the Russians, not looking unduly concerned, picked up bits of broken glass and continued dancing.

Then the cruise director announced, "Ladies and gentlemen, there's nothing to be alarmed about." This was enough to make Noeline alarmed "at what we were supposed not to be alarmed about", and when she and her sister-in-law saw that some people had lifejackets they decided they should return to their cabins and get dressed in something more sensible. A stewardess helped them into lifejackets and told them to go out on to the deck, where they waited.

Geoffrey Naughton, also at the wine tasting, listened intently to the sound the ship made on impact. From his Antarctic research days he was familiar with the sound of pack ice grating along a ship's hull. This sound was familiar, but more metallic, and it started at the front of the ship and ran along what seemed to be the entire length of the hull.

Geoffrey felt the almost immediate list to starboard, and went quickly out on deck. He could see clearly the *Lermontov's* wake fanning out between the land and some exposed rocks, and guessed that they had been holed by a submerged rock. He didn't imagine the ship would sink. It would be a matter of closing off watertight doors and they would stay afloat, albeit with a list. When was the last time, he asked himself, that a cruise ship had sunk? The *Titanic*?

Australian friends Julie Smith and Julie Dalmazzo were in the bar, looking at photos from the cruise 'pirate night', when they felt the ship scrape and shudder. They grabbed hold of each other's arms. Julie Smith had a claustrophobic urge to be outside, a feeling which was to last for hours, and they headed up to the promenade deck.

But once they got up there they were unsure what to do. A female Russian crew member, speaking furtively, said they should go to their cabins. Julie Smith refused, but her friend said the intention was surely that they go and get their lifejackets. So they raced off downstairs, but were in the wrong part of the ship for direct access to their cabin, which was on level 5, the lowest.

Julie Dalmazzo was very frightened. They went upstairs, and reorientated themselves. They passed Irene, the woman who cleaned their cabins, and ignored her advice against going to their cabin. On level 5, one of the automatic doors slowly shut. At the same time an alarm sounded. There was someone on the other side, and the two women part-hoped, part-assumed, that they had a way out. By this time Julie Dalmazzo was hyperventilating, and neither of them knew how to reach a deck again. They didn't try any longer to find their cabin, but discovered a crew's stairway which took them up and onto the promenade deck.

Three bells sounded, but the two friends expected seven, which meant lifeboat drill. An Australian crewman, noticing them on deck, ushered them inside again. But Julie Smith found that stifling, and they returned outside. There they sat, already bracing themselves at an unnatural angle on the high port side, where their assigned lifeboats were. At that point, though Russian crew were racing about, they were the only passengers waiting.

In the shower, Joan Dillon was thrown violently against the wall. She heard loud scraping noises from beneath her feet, and picked herself up, shaken and confused. In the cabin her daughter was bemused and then sharply alarmed by the impact.

Mrs Dillon dressed hastily and together they hurried to the Bolshoi Lounge.

On the other side of the ship, Harry and Jean Thomas were getting themselves ready for dinner. Mrs Thomas was about to step into her shower when the ship struck. Her husband, relaxing on his bunk, quickly jumped to his feet. Through the porthole he could see dirty, disturbed water. It was obvious to him that something had gone seriously wrong.

He grabbed his binoculars, told his wife he'd find out what was happening, and hurried out on deck to have a closer look. He was sure the ship must have hit something. But there was only the grey-green sea and a small yellowish patch of water immediately behind the ship.

Other passengers were hurrying past, wearing or carrying lifejackets, and Harry went quickly back to their cabin to get Jean. She was out of the shower, frightened, dressed for dinner, but wondering whatever was happening. What her husband told her wasn't reassuring.

"Get some sensible clothes on, and those flat shoes, and grab your lifejacket – it looks like the ship could be in trouble," he instructed. Harry also changed into warmer clothes, and put his treasured binoculars away safely in a cupboard before picking up his own lifejacket. When they got to the upper deck one of the stewards directed them to the growing crowd in the Bolshoi Lounge.

People making their way towards the lounge were trying to find out what had happened, but the Russian crew, some already wearing lifejackets, couldn't or wouldn't understand them and were unable to help.

Stewards busied themselves picking up broken glasses and mopping the spilt wine. Others, English-speaking, tried to assure people there was nothing to worry about, but they looked as anxious as the passengers.

At last an announcement over the public address system told the passengers there was no cause for alarm as the ship "has a good captain and a good crew and they will fix the problem shortly". These words became branded in the memories of many of those listening.

Lorand Loblay had been playing chess against his computer in his Tamara Suite on the upper deck. Lorand, born in Transylvania, had seen much upheaval in Europe in the middle years of the century. He had fought in the Soviet Union army, been an interpreter in prisoner-of-war camps, and had experienced life – and near death – in the Russian Gulags.

He was qualified in law and held a master's degree in music, but after settling in Australia he had built up a successful carrier business. He had inspected the *Mikhail Lermontov* during one of its visits to Sydney, and had chosen Tamara, one of the four available suites on the upper deck, for himself and his partner. Lorand found the *Lermontov* to be a well-appointed vessel; no *Queen Elizabeth II*, but a boat the crew were proud of.

When the ship struck, Lorand felt a strong jolt, followed by a scraping noise. His chess pieces fell onto the floor. He was annoyed rather than frightened – annoyed at being so rudely interrupted, and at not being able to reinstate his chess position. He went to the Bolshoi Lounge, but no one there knew what had happened.

Fluent in several European languages, Lorand Loblay understood Russian. He soon realised the ship had hit a reef. Over the public address system he could hear the captain and senior officers summoning key personnel to the bridge, while other crew members were told to go to their emergency stations.

At this stage Lorand was unconcerned for his safety. He couldn't imagine a large ship like the *Lermontov* sinking after what appeared, at the moment, to be a minor mishap.

No information had been given in English over the public

address system. This in no way surprised Lorand. He was familiar with the psyche of the Russian people as well as their language and knew the mentality which pervaded the communist Soviet system.

He knew that making decisions without directions from one's superiors was distinctly politically unwise in the Soviet Union. Errors of judgment, mistakes, loss of face, were likely to cost the 'guilty' party dearly.

Any accident meant a loss of face. That meant that planes never crashed in the Soviet Union, coal mines never exploded, ships never sank. In fact, untold disasters occurred over the years of Soviet communism. But that's what they literally were – untold. The world didn't get to hear about them.

Lorand Loblay completely understood the Russian captain's reluctance to tell the passengers what was happening. Russia might be far away from New Zealand, but under the Soviet regime extremely harsh punishments, seemingly out of all proportion to any 'error', could await those responsible for such a public event as the crippling, or loss, of a ship. 'Errors' shouldn't be hinted at, let alone broadcast.

Even in the day to day running of the ship, the paranoia of communism raised its head. The crew were forbidden, officially, anyway, to associate with the passengers.

The entertainment manager, Australian Lee Young, who was at the wine tasting with his group of performers, had found that even in his position as an employee of the CTC shipping company he couldn't socialise with the Russian crew, or go ashore with them. He was among those to whom Lorand Loblay's summation of the position would have made perfect sense.

In the Bolshoi Lounge, Lorand and his companion met up with their dinner partners during the cruise, John and June Muncy. John Muncy, a retired ship's captain, had taken part in convoys to England in World War II. Lorand was surprised to see the couple wearing their lifejackets.

"I speak from experience," John replied. "This ship has been opened up like a can of sardines."

Still thinking it to be an unnecessary precaution, Lorand

nonetheless fetched two lifejackets.

None of the passengers he saw looked concerned, and in the time-honoured tradition of the *Titanic*, the band played on.

In cabin 545, mid-way along the Baltic deck on the starboard side, the Leihn family had been relaxing after their busy day. The sudden thump and the violent rolling motion of the ship had woken Steven. The two adults looked at each other over the heads of their grandsons, but said nothing. "Come on," Ray said, trying not to sound alarmed, "let's go and see what's happening."

They left the cabin, Lorna Leihn in front, then the two boys, with Ray bringing up the rear. Suddenly, and without any warning, one of the big doors across the corridor slid shut with a hiss of compressed air behind Mrs Leihn, leaving her husband and the two boys on the other side.

For a blood-chilled moment she stood still, wondering why this had happened and whatever she could do. Then desperately she ran down the corridor for help, trying to suppress her rising panic, and wondering if any second another door would suddenly slam shut, trapping her.

Who could help her? Something had gone wrong with the ship, that much she knew. But what had happened to Ray and the boys? Where were they now? Were they all right?

She almost ran into a Russian stewardess in her haste but all her efforts to explain what had happened got her nowhere. The stewardess insisted Mrs Leihn should go immediately to her emergency station, and, when she hesitated, grabbed the frantically protesting woman and hustled her up a nearby stairwell to an upper deck.

Ray Leihn and the boys had hurried back along the frighteningly sloping corridor to their cabin. There, to Ray's horror, they found the portholes were already under water. He was beginning to become deeply afraid. Lorna was God knows where, and probably in a panic, little Steven was crying, and John was screaming. "Pa, we're going to drown!" he cried.

At that moment a Russian crewman rushed into the cabin.

"Out, quickly! Get your lifejackets. You must take the children to the upper deck, quick, quick!"

Ray wanted to stop to lock the cabin door because all their valuables were in there. He had his wallet and a packet of cigarettes in his pocket but everything else was in their cases. "We have no time to lock cabin. Quick – you must go now," the crewman said urgently. They hurried after him, Ray half dragging Steven and shunting John along ahead of him while all the time he looked for Lorna.

In the Bolshoi Lounge the boys spotted their grandmother, and shouted to her, and they were quickly all reunited, the adults taking huge breaths of relief and trying to make out that the whole thing was an adventure, to calm the boys. After the urgency used to get them out of their cabin they were amazed at the relaxed air in the lounge. Music was still playing and some people were drinking again, in spite of the distinctly sloping floor.

The stewards were encouraging the wine-tasting to continue but only those who decided they needed a drink, any kind of drink to establish some kind of normality, were interested. Nobody wanted to debate, now, the finer points of wine.

Wal and Jean Thorpe had been playing table tennis with a small group of friends in the gym deck near the stern of the ship. The extraordinary jolt had brought their game to a halt.

Wal rushed to the starboard side of the ship to look back at the passage the ship had just come through, where its wake showed as a big dirty white smudge on the dark sea. Turning to Jean in disbelief, he said, "I wouldn't take even a small boat through there."

Down in the bowels of the ship, near the main cool stores, refrigeration engineer Parvee Zagliadimov and four other crew members had been helping to prepare for the night's dinner party. Trolleys of foodstuffs had already been selected from the frozen stores to take to the galley for the cooks.

The men had been joking and laughing together. The after-dinner dancing and music would amuse the elderly passengers for a while but there was no possibility of romance there. One of the hostesses, however, had caught the engineer's eye, and he was looking forward to the evening's fun. Life had been lonely since his divorce.

"Leave the vodka alone tonight, Parvee, or you will only be good for singing songs to her and she might like something a little more memorable after the dance," one of the others teased him.

"I'll leave you to guess about that. I've got work to do next door in the compressor room before tonight," Parvee laughed, and disappeared as he shut the adjoining door behind him.

Minutes later, it happened. With a tremendous crack and a roar, the heavy trolleys were thrown against the door. The deck heaved, and the scream of tortured steel drowned out all other noise.

The four remaining men were suddenly knee-deep in water. It came gushing through the compartment with enough force to knock them off balance. Reeling from the impact, the crewmen rushed for the ladder leading up to the next deck.

The trolleys had jammed shut the door to the compressor room. They would never know if their shouted warnings to Parvee were even heard.

On the bridge Captain Vorobyov was momentarily disorientated. It had stopped raining and he could clearly see the Cape Jackson lighthouse. But it should have been on his port side and two miles astern. Instead it was about 300 metres away to starboard. They were between the sharp rocks of the cape and the lighthouse, when they should have been well out in Cook Strait.

What were they doing in here? What the hell had his senior officers done, letting the pilot bring his ship in so close – after he had warned them?

Someone had ordered "Stop engines" on the engine room telegraph, and ordered the helmsman to steer to port. It was clear to the captain that for the moment there was little more he could do.

The furious Russian master turned to the stricken pilot. "What has happened?"

"I don't know," came the reply. It was obvious Captain Jamison had not gathered his thoughts, and was stunned.

He was standing on the port side of the wheelhouse, obviously in shock. Second mate Gusev was ashen. Chief navigator Stepanishchev, who had been the most senior of the Russian officers on the bridge, was shaken and white-faced.

"The pilot recommended I should allow him to take the ship through the pass to give the passengers a good look at Cape Jackson and the lighthouse. He assured me it was safe to do so," he managed to stammer.

Orders and questions were piling up on each other in English and Russian. Don Jamison, paradoxically still the man with the best local knowledge, pulled himself together and made a practical decision. He used the VHF radio to call Picton Harbour Radio to tell them what had happened and to say that assistance might be needed.

"This is a Mayday situation, the *Mikhail Lermontov*," he told them. "We have struck a rock at Cape Jackson and we are proceeding into Port Gore to assess the damage. Will you please advise Wellington we will need emergency services."

CHAPTER FOUR

Rescuers Gather

ON THE BRIDGE of the rail ferry *Arahura*, some 35 kilometres away to the south-east, Captain John Brew steadied his ship as she rounded Heaphy Point, scanning ahead through the late afternoon glare. A heavily overcast sky and low sun made naked eye visibility unreliable. But, in the close confines of Tory Channel, and as he had done on so many hundreds of previous trips to Picton, he was looking carefully for small boats or anything else he might need to avoid.

In another five minutes this New Zealand Railways inter-island ferry would leave Tory Channel to enter Queen Charlotte Sound, and turn to port for the final run to Picton harbour, following the same path the cruise ship had taken on its way into Picton earlier that day.

Then, suddenly, Wellington Radio came on air. There seemed to be a ship in trouble. Everyone on the bridge listened intently, with Captain Brew straining his ears to catch every word.

He could hear only half the conversation because the steep-sided Sounds made radio transmissions difficult to receive. "This is Wellington Radio. Do I understand you have a Mayday situation?" he heard. Then there was silence except for static interference.

Captain Brew was concerned at the use of the word Mayday – the international distress call.

Wellington Radio repeated its call, mentioning Cape Jackson. Captain Brew unhesitatingly spoke to Wellington Radio to say he was a few minutes away from Queen Charlotte Sound where he was due to turn to port away from the ship in trouble. He could instead turn to starboard and give assistance if required.

Wellington Radio acknowledged his call and asked him to stand by. But no further message for him came.

Now the airwaves were full of ships and shore stations

responding to the apparent distress call. People wanted to know what was going on, while others were offering assistance. Captain Brew could hear only some of the calls and had no clear idea what was happening, except that there seemed to be a large passenger ship in trouble not far away. He had to make a decision. He hadn't heard from Wellington Radio or the troubled ship, but it was better to be heading for the area where he might be needed rather than steaming away from it.

As they cleared Tory Channel he decided. "Starboard fifteen," he ordered quietly.

"Starboard fifteen, sir," his helmsman replied.

The high-sided shallow-drafted ferry heeled over and swung her nose up Queen Charlotte Sound towards Cook Strait and the unnamed ship in trouble.

"Ease to five," Captain Brew ordered as she neared her new course, and called the engineer to start the fourth engine. The ship usually had one of her four engines out of operation for routine maintenance, but he would need all the speed he could get if there was an emergency.

He made an announcement over the public address system to tell his passengers what was happening. They would be late for appointments, or other transport connections. Some of them would undoubtedly be annoyed at the unexpected change of plans. They needed to know what he was doing, and to be kept informed.

With the fourth engine now running, the *Arahura* increased her speed from the usual 18 knots to her full 22 knots. Spray flew over her high bows. The crew had been alerted and everyone waited to see what troubles lay ahead. This was an adventurous departure from the ferry's normal routine. Some of the crew relished the urgency, which seemed to increase each time the ship smashed her bows into another sea.

Out at Cape Jackson, David Baker, a 36-year-old farmer, had earlier watched the big Russian passenger liner steaming up Queen Charlotte Sound. He had remarked to his cousin. Denis Cox, who was visiting the remote Cape Jackson farm, how unusual it was for big ships to be on the western side of

Motuara Island.

Large ships generally avoided the area, as the number of reefs and areas of foul ground were well known and were included on all marine navigation charts. Such ships usually steamed through in the deep water on the far side of Motuara Island, but this ship was so close to the shoreline as she passed the Baker farm that she almost disappeared from view under the headland near Waihi Point, just past the bay where the Bakers had their small jetty.

David farmed the 1500-hectare property with his parents, Tony and Betty Baker, who operated the renowned voluntary VHF radio service for local fishermen and pleasure boat skippers.

Over the years Cape Jackson Radio had become a unique Sounds institution. It had developed from a casual hobby to a full-time occupation, particularly in the summer months when hundreds of holidaymakers took to the water in a colourful variety of small motor boats and yachts. The Bakers' knowledge of their waters was legendary, as was their generous sharing of this knowledge. For help of any kind, boaties looked to the Bakers.

The two Baker farmhouses, situated on the narrow tongue of steep land that separated the northern entrance to Queen Charlotte Sound from the bay called Port Gore to the west, were in an ideal location for a radio and lookout service. Some five miles to the north the rugged narrow landform culminated in Cape Jackson, and a quarter of a mile off shore stood its lighthouse on its tiny pinnacle of rock.

As they did with all ships, the Bakers had exchanged radio greetings with Don Jamison aboard the *Mikhail Lermontov*, and had remarked among themselves how striking the big white ship looked against the spectacular scenery of the Sounds. The Bakers knew there was plenty of depth where the pilot was taking the ship, provided she kept away from Motuara Island.

They had chatted until the ship steamed out of view. Don Jamison had said he was giving the passengers a sightseeing tour of the Sounds on the way out, and was taking a course on the near side of the island so they could see Cape Jackson and the lighthouse. He'd said it was a shame about the weather and hoped it would improve.

Then, not long after the ship had passed out of sight of both the Baker homesteads, David Baker heard a most unusual noise, like metal grinding, and phoned his father who dismissed the notion. Almost immediately, it seemed, the Bakers had then heard the electrifying radio call from Don Jamison.

The Russian ship had hit something at Cape Jackson. They were going to take the ship into Port Gore to assess the damage, they heard.

The Bakers regarded the sea beyond the farm as more or less their own, and took a proprietary interest in what happened on and in it. Betty Baker felt personally involved, and distressed that the beautiful ship she had just seen passing through her domain should have come to some kind of harm. She hoped it wasn't serious.

There were to be hundreds of radio calls for the Bakers to receive and pass on during the next exhausting 36 hours, while they acted as a link between stations unable to contact each other directly because of the way the steep hills interfered with their radio signals.

David Baker and his cousin Denis were sitting down to a quick evening meal of scrambled eggs when his parents called him – the cruise ship that had earlier passed their farm had hit something. She could be in serious trouble. David at once thought of that noise. He and Denis finished their meal rapidly and went to see what they could do.

That first radio message Betty Baker heard turned out to be the start of the most frustrating of the hundreds of rescue operations which the family had helped co-ordinate over the years. It was the first where essential assistance was stubbornly declined until it was almost too late to save lives.

For hours on end all the radio messages to the stricken ship, messages seeking vital information for the rescue operation, would be ignored or misunderstood.

Nearly 40 kilometres away to the west, Captain John Reedman on the LPG tanker *Tarihiko* had also heard what he thought was a Mayday call. The tanker often waited in the shelter of d'Urville Island before the final run to the North Island, to New Plymouth, to collect a cargo of the highly volatile gas, and then on to northern ports. Anchoring in the Sounds was not as costly as waiting berthed in New Plymouth. When the ship was ahead of schedule, the 18-man crew usually spent this time relaxing or doing maintenance, but the radio call promised some excitement.

John Reedman told First Mate Rod Theobold to have the anchors lifted while he called Wellington Radio for information. At first he'd thought the message had come from a trawler in trouble but a check of his radio call sign list showed this was a large passenger liner. "It could be all on here," he told the mate.

Then he spoke to Wellington Radio more formally, using the almost dictation speed and deliberate clarity needed to ensure messages got through. "I am about one and a half hours' steaming away from the passenger ship. We are standing by if you need any assistance."

He listened intently to the tangle of radio messages and was concerned to hear the troubled ship was already listing to starboard. Right then he decided to head for Port Gore immediately, without waiting for instructions. He hoped he could get more information on the way.

David Baker had spent his boyhood at Cape Jackson and knew the rugged coastline intimately. He'd learned to row small boats in the sheltered bays and had dived and fished over most of it. He'd grown up with a healthy respect for the sea and knew the dangers of taking risks in the Sounds. He was therefore astonished that such a large vessel would attempt such a passage.

Smaller vessels often went through the gap but they were generally skippered by experienced people who knew the nature and times of the local tides, and where the clear water was. Although sea currents raged and crashed over the submerged reefs in the passage in heavy weather, on windless days the area was a favoured fishing spot.

David and Denis, with David's 11-year-old son Jason, took a hand-held radio set to listen in to the drama, and rode farm bikes to the top of the hill near the homestead. They watched, disbelieving, as the ship appeared through the rain on the far side of Cape Jackson. She was listing to starboard and steaming slowly.

Radio messages were now being broadcast with increasing intensity. They heard Captain Brew on the *Arahura*, bound for Picton, asking if his help was needed, and Wellington Radio's response that few details were known but that the *Arahura* should stand by. They heard Captain Reedman on the *Tarihiko*, and listened in disbelief as Wellington Radio cut in to say that no help was required.

They almost cheered when the message was ignored and the *Tarihiko* said it was changing course for Port Gore. David, Denis and Jason decided to go to the farmhouse, wondering what would be unfolding out of sight in the bay below the farm, and what could be done to help.

David heard the Russians decline initial offers of assistance. This seemed unbelievable. He couldn't feel at all certain that the ship would survive. He'd never seen such a large ship in trouble. In this case, too, he knew most of its passengers would be elderly and already distressed, and he simply couldn't understand why those on board had rejected offers of help. As the three rode their bikes along the ridge to keep the stricken ship in view, they felt shocked and powerless.

Now fishing boat skippers and small boat owners, alerted by friends if they hadn't had their radios on, were starting to call in, seeking information.

Tony Baker had called Wellington Radio again to see what help was required but was told the Russian captain did not want assistance. Tony certainly wasn't satisfied with the response and called the Wellington-based fishing industry station, Cobar Radio, and spoke to operator Ron Smith. "Sooner or later that ship is going to need help but nobody seems to be doing anything about it," he said. Ron Smith agreed.

Talking it over, the Bakers decided to call up Captain Brian Pickering, the senior representative of the Marine Department in Picton. They described the situation as best they understood it. Would he bring the habour board boat, the *Enterprise*, to help? But again the fact that there was no Mayday meant the Marine Department wouldn't agree.

The Bakers began calling local boats by radio, and other Sounds fishermen on the telephone. "To hell with Wellington Radio. That big Russian is in trouble and we better get out there damn quick," one skipper called back.

At home on Arapawa Island, Joe Heberley had heard the *Mikhail Lermontov's* distress call on VHF radio. He wondered "what the hell was going on". Joe lived at Okukari Bay on Arapawa Island just inside the Heads, the narrow entrance from Cook Strait into Tory Channel. Arapawa Island formed the East Head.

He was the experienced head of Search and Rescue for the area. With his sons Joe and James, all of them farmers as well as fishermen, he had been involved in what seemed innumerable searches and rescues at sea, though never anything on this scale.

He called the Bakers to see what was happening. Although the cruise ship had refused assistance, Joe and sons Joe and James left for Port Gore before they were officially called out. They knew the sooner they were on the spot the better. Joe's wife, Heather Heberley, had taken part in many rescues. This time she stayed behind in case the space she took aboard their fishing boat, the *Fugitive*, was needed by a survivor off the ship.

Some of the fishing boats heading for Port Gore were several hours' steaming from the scene, but if Cape Jackson Radio said they were needed, they knew they were.

Obviously Wellington Radio couldn't know what was really happening.

On the bridge of the *Mikhail Lermontov*, radio messages and questions from senior officers had been coming thick and fast.

"Picton Harbour Radio calling us, sir. What assistance do we need?"

"Shall I alert the passengers and get them into lifejackets, sir?"

"Message from the inter-island ferry *Arahura* out from Wellington, sir. She will divert from Picton if we want help."

"Shall I prepare the passengers to abandon ship, sir?"

The bubble of indecision finally burst. "No. By God you will not!" the captain said. He ordered the engines full ahead and turned the ship to starboard and open water away from the reef.

His ship was listing and had obviously sustained serious damage below the waterline. Captain Vorobyov ordered the emergency stations alarm to be sounded and went out onto the port bridge wing to look astern. A huge swirling patch of yellow-brown water still showed, where they had hit the reef.

Staff Captain Georgey Melnik, who was responsible for damage control, didn't wait for more instructions but sounded the general emergency alarm for the crew. His four well-drilled teams swung quickly into action, bringing reports from everywhere below the water line.

This information confirmed that the ship was taking water fast, and was in grave danger. There was major flooding above the storage tank tops and below the waterline in between frames 107 and 175. All crew in these areas were quickly evacuated.

"Captain, we have flooding in the four main watertight divisions. The crew have been evacuated and the doors closed. All available pumps are working to capacity and we should be able to confine the flooding to that area, but she still won't stay afloat, sir," Georgey Melnik reported.

Don Jamison finally caught the Russian master's attention and asked him what assistance he needed. "I want a tug boat to help us beach the ship," he was told. "I don't want assistance to take the passengers off. We are not going to abandon ship out here."

Captain Vorobyov was over the shock of realising that the pilot had grounded his ship on rocks, putting them in such serious trouble. He had moved from shock to anger. He was more furious than he could ever recall having been. Some of his fury he directed at himself – he had reprimanded the pilot earlier in the day for taking the ship too close to the shore, but he himself was the man ultimately responsible. He should have stayed on the bridge until the end of pilotage limits, and relieved Jamison immediately.

Holy Jesus, he wondered, *how did I allow my ship to get into this mess?* He had known deep inside it was risky. He'd also known he could have, and should have, forbidden any repeat of the Shakespeare Bay incident. Now he had a crippled ship in foreign waters and hundreds of lives in danger.

Those around him were aware of his fury. He did not, however, let his anger blind him to what must be done, and done quickly. Turning to the pilot, who had by now got over his own initial shock, he invited him to the forepart of the bridge. "Where can I find a safe beach to run her aground?" he demanded.

The two professional seamen knew they had to work together if they were going to save the ship. Recriminations – everything else – could wait until later. There was no time to think about these now. Some things were happening too rapidly, others weren't happening fast enough.

"There's a sandy shallow beach at the south end of Port Gore, sir. A policeman in Picton and the skipper of one of these small boats in the bay have confirmed it's the best we're likely to get."

"Good. We should make that if we take it carefully," the captain replied.

Captain Jamison now sent to Picton Harbour Radio the message that the Russian master didn't want to hear, and which had every radio operator within listening range on full alert. "The vessel is in danger of sinking, vessel in danger of sinking. We are making water and proceeding into Port Gore, over," he said.

Wellington Radio picked up the message and called to see how serious the situation was. Don Jamison repeated the message. He suggested to Captain Vorobyov that they could go out around the Cape Jackson lighthouse and return to Ship Cove, instead of carrying on into Port Gore. The Russian master decided to continue on the present heading. He did however follow Don Jamison's suggestion to head for Tunnel Bay where two buildings near the beach would provide navigation points.

Captain Vorobyov ordered slow ahead to reduce the flow of water through the hole in the hull while she swung to port. When the ship was pointed between the two buildings he brought her back up to full ahead again. He was trying to be optimistic. The ship's electronic systems were beginning to fail and passengers were nervous, but if he could get the ship safely beached he could put them ashore. If they were forced to abandon ship in deep water, who knew what would happen? Most of the passengers were elderly. They would not survive long if they fell into the water of this apparently uninhabited large bay.

Horrie Dargie was a harmonica player, one of the 25 entertainers whose cabin accommodation was the same as the passengers'. Earlier he had been attending the wine tasting in the Bolshoi Lounge and having a pleasant time. The company was great and the food was good – too good. Horrie and his wife Kathy had put themselves on a Weight Watchers diet. A fellow entertainer, the singer-comedienne Bunny Gibson, had been teasing him about the cream cakes they'd had for lunch. "I'll get you yet, Bunny!" he threatened.

At that very moment the ship had lurched.

"That was a bit sudden, Horrie!" Bunny responded.

Paul Maybury, another entertainer, said "D'you know what that reminded me of? A scene from that movie about the *Titanic*!"

But the wine tasting carried on, and not until the public address system announced there was nothing to be alarmed about did Bunny wonder if that meant there *was* something to be alarmed about.

She noticed the deck had begun to list. Would they still be performing that night? Would that affect their act?

"You'd do anything to get out of working tonight, wouldn't you, Bunny?" Paul said.

Still joking, they decided to go to the bar for a 'real drink', and had fun with their glasses continually sliding along the bar.

On the way out of the lounge, Bunny had happened to look down the stairwell that spiralled round and round right to the bottom deck. She could see water swirling. After their drinks she looked again. The Russian crew had strung a tarpaulin over the water to hide it – but water was swirling up over it.

Back in the Bolshoi Lounge they saw the list had got worse. There was another announcement: would everybody please hold on to something solid, because the captain was going to run the ship aground. There would be another jolt. Again there was no cause for alarm – oh, and dinner would be half an hour late.

Noeline Rodger and Audrey Peterson obeyed the order. "We hung on like mad," she was to say later, "but nothing happened and still nothing happened. Some of the crew had big plastic bags of bread and tins of fish which they were trying to bring up on to the deck. But the passengers were so scared they wouldn't let go, to let the men through. Some of the younger women on the cruise helped – they were really good, bringing blankets and helping older people through the passageways."

Eventually they returned to the Bolshoi Lounge.

Noeline particularly noticed the fortitude of the many elderly people. It wasn't surprising, she thought. After all, they had been through a depression and a war, and had become philosophical. She realised she herself was thinking, "If I drown, I drown."

Among the impressive people who were now unobtrusively joking and calming anyone who looked particularly apprehensive, Clare Stevenson stood out. Noeline had earlier met and admired her. Both had wide experience in voluntary work, and Noeline happened to know that Clare, like many of the passengers, had decided against taking out insurance for the voyage. That was because medical treatment on the cruise ship was free, and people thought they would simply carry their luggage on, and carry it off again at the other end.

Now Noeline said to her, "I'm sorry about this, Clare."

"It's an old dog for a hard road," Clare Stevenson said, almost cheerfully.

Another Aucklander, a popular, whimsical Irishman called Bill Cook, told the group he had no insurance either. "Well," he said, "I'm going to get my $40 departure tax back!"

Outside on the promenade deck, the two Julies, Smith and Dalmazzo, had by now been joined by other passengers. They found lifejackets stored inside the benches on the deck and put them on. Julie Smith heard British members of the CTC staff advising, in suave accents, that there was no danger, and would passengers wait in the lounges, please. She heard the cruise director's voice: "There won't be as many courses as usual, and our waiters and waitresses might not be in uniform, but please, do go down to dinner." Julie, and no one near her, moved.

The band continued to play, in spite of the difficulty they were now having holding on to their instruments on the increasingly sloping stage.

Everyone knew what had happened to the *Titanic*, and many had seen the old movie about its sinking, A Night To Remember, the movie made many years before Spielberg's blockbuster version.

But the *Mikhail Lermontov* was surely different, a modern, fully equipped ship, totally different from the *Titanic*. They were so close to land, and of course there were no icebergs.

In one corner of the Bolshoi Lounge a foursome was intent on their game of bridge, concentrating hard and seeming to ignore the commotion going on about them. But the starboard list was noticeable, and more of the passengers gathering in the lounge were now wearing their lifejackets.

Clare Stevenson was laughing heartily, sharing a joke with one of the crew and taking care that others nearby were caught up by her infectious laughter, and starting to smile themselves. But she was thinking hard, thinking back to her old training and experience.

Clare liked to say she was a former WAAAF, but she was no ordinary former servicewoman. In fact she had been director of the Women's Auxiliary Australian Air Force from the early days of World War Two. By war's end she was the most senior officer of all four women's services with the Australian Defence Forces.

Now she was taking in the implications of the situation, and seeing where she could give a lead: *you may be scared, but don't show it.* She appeared calm and totally in control of events around her, dressed for the evening's entertainment. But she had let one of the younger passengers put a cumbersome lifejacket on her, and moved quietly from group to group, speaking matter-of-factly about its being commonsense to put on lifejackets, "just in case".

Joan Dillon and Gail had returned hastily to their cabin and filled travel bags with their more valuable possessions, then returned to the lounge. On the way they noticed that the ship was listing more. Then, as they passed a stairwell, they saw water gushing below. The fact that crew had tried to hide this terrifying sight with a tarpaulin made it even worse.

Harry and Jean Thomas found the noise and adrenalin levels within the lounge overwhelming, and decided to go up to the viewing balcony outside, where it was quieter. Harry, who had a heart condition, searched his pockets for one of his tablets, which he placed under his tongue.

Mark Raymond had remained in his seat, but was becoming more uneasy. He had decided against going to his cabin to gather his belongings, although by now he was convinced the ship was in grave trouble. He eventually admitted to himself that he was frightened, but knew he shouldn't show it. It wouldn't take much for panic to spread. Some of the elderly passengers were already quite fearful, and Mark noticed many were holding hands and trying to comfort each other.

He decided he should wait until there was an announcement for people to gather their things together. That instruction never came.

Now, among the many messages in Russian over the public address system, there came an announcement in English that the first sitting for dinner would be delayed. The Leihn boys were disappointed. There were to be T-bone steaks that night and they were "starving" again.

A second announcement assured them there was nothing to worry about, and they could take their lifejackets off if they wanted to.

Ray Leihn had also looked down a stairwell and seen water two decks below. There was no way his family were taking their lifejackets off. He and Lorna decided they and the boys would all hold hands to avoid being separated again until they got to safety.

Mark Raymond had finally accepted that the passengers in the Bolshoi Lounge should not wait for instructions to put on lifejackets. Many had been wearing them when they came in but those who had been at the abandoned wine-tasting were still waiting for instructions. The ship was obviously going to sink, he believed, even though by now there had been an announcement that the ship was going to be beached. They had all been told to sit down, to avoid being injured, before the ship was run aground. But time ticked on and nothing happened.

He was one of only a handful of younger passengers on board. The rest were quite old or were children. Some grandparents were travelling with several children, although none as young as the Leihn boys. With three of the other younger passengers, Mark began helping those around him into their heavy lifejackets.

Mark tried to imagine all the things that might happen. He was seriously concerned for the old people and smaller children. He had looked out the window and was sure he could swim to the shore if he had to, but most of the other passengers would have difficulty. And it was beginning to get dark. New Zealand's famous long white cloud, possibly meaning a long twilight to the Polynesians whose tropical dusks and dawns were abrupt, was not infinite. What would happen, he wondered, when it was fully dark?

Two of the passengers who had joined the *Mikhail Lermontov* in Picton were Eric and Phyllis Wilkes, old friends of the pilot, Don Jamison.

Eric had been shipwrecked during service in World War Two, and had long thought about taking another, and more agreeable, sea journey. Bringing his wife on this cruise had seemed just the thing. Besides, they would be able to relax with Don Jamison when he wasn't piloting. To be shipwrecked for the second time, and before he'd even left his own Marlborough Sounds, wasn't something which had crossed his mind for a moment.

Now husband and wife sat quietly, deeply and gravely concerned. The noise, the apprehension levels, the total uncertainty, affected Phyllis Wilkes. She needed a soft drink.

A Russian steward, a glass of lemonade on a tray, came to her down the alarmingly sloping floor. This son of communism held out his hand. "That will be a dollar fifty."

Of all the stories which so soon were to rush around the world, this incident – certainly to many Picton people – may have been the most remarkable of them all.

Geoffrey Naughton had returned from the deck to sit, braced, against the bulkhead just aft of the Bolshoi Lounge. The sitting and waiting seemed to go on for a long time, until he felt the *Lermontov* slowly drift to a stop, and saw that the crew were beginning to organise people into some form of grouping, ready to abandon ship.

At that point Geoffrey became anxious about collecting some of his belongings. His cabin was above the water line, and he thought there was no point in returning to it as the watertight doors would be closed. But one of the announcements made him think that, if he hurried, he should be able to get there and back safely.

In his cabin he collected his wallet and passport. He had expensive camera gear with him, but knew from previous lifeboat drills that you don't load yourself up with things –

just warm clothing, and maybe some food, was enough. And besides, he still didn't think the ship would sink. He went back up the stairs.

Tom Archer, one of the elderly passengers Mark Raymond was so concerned about, was indeed anxious, but for another, more immediate and personal reason. A Russian crewman had told his group they were to go immediately to their lifeboat station on D deck, but Tom desperately needed to go to the toilet.
Several glasses of beer and two or three of wine had taken their effect, and, sinking ship or not, he had to go. Telling his wife and sister to wait for him he hurried across the sloping floor to the gents.
When he turned to come out, the door had jammed. Try as he might he simply could not open it.
He hammered on the door and shouted. Nobody came. *"What a bloody place to end up in!"* he thought. He gave the door an extra savage kick, just under the catch – and it flew open.
Back in the lounge his anxious wife and sister-in-law were still waiting. "I got stuck in the bloody dunny!" he announced, loudly enough for others to hear – to his wife's embarrassment. They set off along the sloping floor to the stairs.
Entertainer Paul Maybury stayed with two young women passengers, to help with getting the older people ready to abandon ship.

Lee Young kept up people's spirits with a stream of quips. To one elderly Sydney woman he said, "Don't worry, tomorrow you'll be a star on the front page of the *Mirror*."
"Thank God," she replied. "We'll get Lindy Chamberlain off the front page."
One young male passenger had earlier come to Lee's notice as he had a slight limp. When he came to help him down a rope ladder, Lee found he actually had only one leg.
Lee also observed, time and again, that the previously socially aloof Russian crew were fantastic, behaving

impeccably and with warmth and concern for all passengers.

Geoffrey Naughton was also quietly helping, staying with an elderly woman who needed two walking sticks to move. He placed her in a queue which extended across the lounge to the doors onto the starboard deck, and entrusted her to a crew member. Then he joined a queue for a lifeboat on the higher port side, where getting into a boat was going to be more difficult. He noted that in this 'for real' lifeboat drill there was no sign of excitement or panic, just a calm curiosity and acceptance.

Harry Thomas had been begging to be allowed to return to his cabin to collect small valuable items. He was particularly anxious to retrieve his main supply of heart tablets. At last he and Jean were told they could go. They struggled along the sloping corridor, walking in the steep V where the floor and the wall met. It didn't seem real. In their cabin they quickly gathered up the tablets and a few other small valuables, and returned to the upper deck.

Wal and Jean Thorpe had delayed going to their cabin. Then, when they'd agreed they really should, they found a steel door barring their way. There was no chance of collecting any of their possessions, and they were dressed in only light clothes.

Robert Diffin decided he wasn't going to leave behind everything he owned. He ignored the instruction for people not to return below to their cabins, and set off. Groping along the deserted sloping corridor in the pitch darkness caused by the ship's worsening electrical problems, he finally located his cabin and managed to get the door open. Inside he fumbled about and found the keys to his Ramsgate Beach home, and his car.

Then he realised it was hopeless and just too dangerous to try to gather anything else, and scrambled back to the emergency ladder and up into the light of the Bolshoi Bar. It had been terrifying in the dark below, but, in his heightened and disoriented state, returning home without his keys had seemed unthinkable.

After the decision was made about 8.30pm to abandon ship,

Lorand Loblay and his companion went to their cabin to grab blankets, passports and jewellery. It was dark, and the list so great it took their combined strength to open the cabin door to get out again.

They started to go to H deck to board a lifeboat, but found much confusion because directions were being passed from passenger to passenger, more like informal rumour than factual information. Word went around that H deck was already under water and they made their way back to the top deck where stations for evacuation were situated. Lorand saw confusion, but no panic.

Bunny Gibson decided she must go and rescue her old, frayed denim cap that she'd had for 12 years. It was her good luck cap. When she got to her F deck cabin, the lights had gone out and she groped around before she found it, and her passport.

She and Horrie and Kathy Dargie – old hands at travel if not at shipwrecks – thought that if they were going to disembark, they'd getter go to the toilet first, in the dark.

An announcement on the public address system said passengers should proceed to H deck, rumours notwithstanding, and as the threesome made their way up they found elderly passengers, who had lost their way, slipping and sliding against the increasing list.

Along with crew members, the entertainers pushed, shoved, and half-carried struggling passengers up the stairs, where Russian sailors picked them up bodily.

In spite of all the commotion, and the angles at which their beds were now tilting, some passengers who had been sleeping when the ship struck, and who had slept through the series of jarring crashes, had to be woken by crew members who were checking every cabin.

Almost unbelievably, some passengers had to be shaken awake.

CHAPTER FIVE

"Assistance Not Required"

ON THE BRIDGE of the *Mikhail Lermontov* a call had come from Wellington Radio. Don Jamison was asked what emergency services were needed. "The situation is stable at the moment, I think," he radioed back.

Other ships were calling in. Don Jamison was sure the ship needed all the assistance he could arrange for her but he couldn't get the Russian master to accept anything other than a tug to push him ashore if he lost power. But there was no tug in the immediate area.

At 6.20pm, about an hour after the ship struck, frustration had turned back to anger between the two men as Captain Vorobyov still refused to confirm his ship was in danger of sinking. All Don Jamison could do was relay the captain's messages of stubborn refusal.

Wellington Radio had finally made contact with Captain Brew on the *Arahura* as he was nearing Motuara Island. "This is Wellington Radio. Your assistance is not required. Repeat, no assistance required. Over." There was a sense of disbelief among his crew as Captain Brew slowed his ship, turned her about and headed back towards Picton. They could still hear radio messages from the cruise ship, which was obviously in some sort of difficulty.

John Brew was very uneasy indeed. The messages going back and forth between the cruise ship, in the outer Sounds, and various other stations, were confused and difficult to understand. He recognised the familiar voice of Don Jamison on the radio, but couldn't make out clearly what was happening. Then other duties demanded his attention, and he concentrated on getting the ferry's passengers and freight to Picton.

Wellington Radio had not been able to make head or tail of

the information they were receiving. They urgently wanted to know exactly what they were dealing with.

"*Mikhail Lermontov* from Wellington Harbour Radio, request you confirm this is a Mayday situation, over," they sent.

Don Jamison again asked Captain Vorobyov, who again firmly refused to accept that the situation must be more fully explained to the wider world. This was not the Russian way. The frustrated pilot could only reply to Wellington Radio, "Negative, no Mayday at present, no Mayday at present," he called. He left the bridge to try to cool down.

Chief engineer Yuri Bolshavok called the bridge to say water was flooding the main electrical switchboard. This was a divided distribution board, either half of which could operate to supply the ship's needs, but water from a crack in the opposite bulkhead was spraying onto both halves. No matter what was being done to try to prevent this, it seemed almost inevitable that they would short-circuit, and soon.

This would cut power to fuel and engine oil pumps. Emergency generators would operate, so there would still be lights in parts of the ship. But the emergency generators wouldn't power the engines. This meant the engines would stop, and the ship would no longer be able to move under her own power. The ship would be helpless without a tug boat to push her ashore. There was no tug boat. And there was no way of telling exactly when this short circuit would occur.

Don Jamison had returned to the bridge in time to hear that the *Tarihiko* was on her way from near d'Urville Island, and that the police launch, *Lady Elizabeth II*, had set out from Wellington.

Wellington Radio again called him to find out what was happening. "We have two questions for you," they said. "Do you still require assistance, and what sort of assistance do you require? And for your information the *Tarihiko* is proceeding to your position at full speed and is on channel 16, over."

Don Jamison called back to say the ship now had a ten degrees list to starboard, and that the Russian captain was heading into Port Gore either to anchor or to run her aground. "We will determine requirements at that stage," he reported.

Again the pilot was obliged to relay the Russian captain's refusal to accept help. "Wellington Radio from *Mikhail Lermontov*. The captain advises me he does not require assistance, he does not require assistance, over."

Captain John Reedman on the *Tarihiko* picked up the message and again chose to ignore it. It was up to him where he took his ship. The side-trip wouldn't use much fuel, and, if his owners objected, he'd deal with that when it happened. He mightn't even be late at his next port. He called Wellington Radio. "I have received that. My intentions are to steam to Port Gore at full speed and have a look, and then proceed to New Plymouth, over."

Chief navigator Stepanishchev had reported the damage-control parties' discovery that some of the watertight doors had sprung under pressure. Water was flooding into new compartments. Now a message came to the bridge from a frantic chief engineer, to say water was entering the engine room and the pumps could not keep up. They must find a safe beach to run her aground, fast. If she went down in deep water they were in all kinds of trouble. Suddenly, that seemed possible.

"How far away is that tug boat? I will need help to keep her on the beach. I will have to ask one of the other ships to help if the tug doesn't get here soon," Vorobyov said, as much to himself as those around him. There was no reply and he didn't really expect one. The ship was now well down by the starboard bow and still taking water.

The main switchboard shorted out. Too much water was coming through the cracks which had appeared in the bulkhead. The situation had not improved, as Captain Vorobyov had hoped it would.

Outside the rain was falling again, the wind had swung to the south-east, and the temperature was dropping. It was after 7pm. The light was beginning to fade. Things were taking a dangerous turn, and his confidence in his ability to save his ship and everyone in her was beginning to waver.

Captain Vorobyov could faintly see the sandy beach, a glimmer in the growing dark, edged with white where the small waves broke. The charts showed deep water up to about 100 metres off shore. If he could get the bow on to the beach and let the anchors go, things would be all right. She would carry on moving in slowly, but she was so deep in the water at the bow that she was making only about four knots. He had to beach the ship.

With a slight lurch, the ship grounded on a sand bar. Could this be the place? Captain Vorobyov believed she was still too far off the shore. Don Jamison suggested they should drop the anchors to hold her there.

He was using the radio to give a running report of events to Picton Harbour Radio where police constable Bill Gibb had been joined by the assistant harbourmaster, Gary Neill. Bill Gibb thought the captain should drop his anchors to hold the ship where she was. "I've already made that suggestion," Don Jamison told him.

Captain Vorobyov hadn't even acknowledged what Jamison had said. He wanted to get the ship closer. If he let his anchors go, he thought some of the passengers might get the idea they would be able to swim ashore. They wouldn't realise they were still in 40 feet of water. There would be casualties. He wanted to get people off under totally controlled conditions. The risk was too great yet.

He asked Don Jamison about the state of the tide and what other measures were being taken to help him save the ship from sinking. Perhaps they could float off the sandbar and get closer in.

"The tide should start rising in about half an hour," Don Jamison told him. "There are two ships from Picton on their way. I don't know what ships they are but they will be here in about two hours."

The list was about 17 degrees but the rate of flooding had steadied so the captain believed the ship would last as long as that, provided nothing else went wrong.

Up to the moment when the ship had nudged on to the sandbar, things on the bridge had seemed settled. Everyone knew what they had to do, and they were going about their tasks with as little fuss as they could. Everything that could be under control was under control. They'd thought that, with any luck, the ship would soon be beached so later she could be repaired and refloated. All the passengers would be safe.

Captain Vorobyov had started to think ahead to salvage operations. He'd asked Captain Jamison to repeat the request for salvage assistance but again declined suggestions that he should send a Mayday distress signal. There was no need for that. The situation was under control.

He decided to start loading passengers into the lifeboats to take them ashore, rather than wait until the ship was beached. Passengers had been mustered in the alleyway between the two main embarkation doors. One of the pair of five-crew tenders, the one from the port side, had been filled first, and had headed for the beach, under the command of Staff Captain Georgey Melnik.

The fear and confusion on the faces of passengers setting off on that first trip would stay with Captain Vorobyov for many years. He knew this. But with any luck, he thought, he would have everyone safely on dry land before the ship grounded. There was no more that he could do for them.

When the tender got to the beach, however, Georgey Melnik was far from confident he could land all the passengers safely. He called the ship. There was only a slight swell breaking on the beach, but the tender might broach and tip passengers into the water. Very conscious of the fact that he was dealing with elderly people, Captain Vorobyov ordered the tender to head for the *Tarihiko* which had now anchored about a quarter of a mile away, further out in the bay. The *Tarihiko* was a relatively small ship, with low sides, so the transfer of passengers would not be too difficult.

The beach seemed so close and the passengers were getting away at a good rate. He was sure he could still save his ship if she carried on moving slowly. He ordered the lifeboats to be manned, then lowered over the side, but to remain secured to the ship as she moved slowly through the water.

Meanwhile, in Picton, Captain Brew had berthed the *Arahura* nearly an hour behind schedule. It was a familiar but highly skilled routine, using rudders, main engines and powerful bow thrusters to turn the ship around inside the confines of Picton harbour, then back it precisely into the specially designed berth so several hundred tonnes of rail wagons could be unloaded. With his senior officers now in charge of loading more rail freight, road vehicles and passengers for the return trip, John Brew hurried ashore to discover what was really happening out near Cape Jackson.

He was still disturbed at having been turned away from the scene when all was obviously not well with the troubled ship. The safety of the people on board was paramount, and he was determined to find out all he could.

In the ferry terminal's radio room he found assistant harbourmaster Gary Neill and constable Bill Gibb, both listening intently to mostly familiar voices. "What's going on out there?" he demanded.

"That Russian liner hit rocks out near Cape Jackson somewhere. It's hard to tell what damage she has but the skipper's turning down all offers of help and only wants a tug to push him on to the beach. It's pretty confused because we can't hear everything," he was told.

This didn't reassure John Brew. "They obviously need help, but Wellington Radio informs me the Rescue Co-ordination Centre says they don't need any," he said.

"Yes, we heard you talking to them. Seems bloody strange to me," Bill Gibb said. He had been a merchant seaman before joining the police in 1970, and understood John Brew's frustration at being turned away from another ship in trouble.

"Hang on, we can call them from here on the phone and find out what the hell they're playing at out there," Bill added, dialling the Wellington number.

"Rescue Co-ordination Centre? Picton Police. Look, we have the *Arahura* here ready to return to Wellington, and several other private vessels are standing by. We can have them in Port Gore in about two hours... What do you mean, they don't want any help? They're sinking! We can hear that from here... A tug boat won't help, and it'd take about three hours to get one there from Wellington..."

The men exchanged baffled looks as the conversation went on. Bill Gibb's tone became more deliberately patient as he decided he was talking to idiots. He spelled the situation out very slowly and clearly.

"Look, all we want is clearance for the *Arahura* to divert from her usual course. She's due to leave here about eight o'clock and will be heading towards Port Gore for about half an hour before she turns into Tory Channel at Dieffenbach Point. After that she'll be steaming away from the area. We also have some other boats standing by to head for the area as soon as you can give us clearance... I don't care what they said, they're obviously in serious trouble out there. Why can't the *Arahura* go and check it out?"

Bill Gibb was frustrated, near to bursting point at the inability of the person on the other end of the line to understand how serious he believed the situation was.

"A waste of bloody time trying to talk to them!" he snorted in disgust when he finally gave up, slamming the phone down and returning to the radio.

When the *Arahura* was ready to sail back to Wellington, confusing radio messages were still being broadcast from the troubled ship. As John Brew headed out of port, the radio messages became more frantic. He could hear other ships in the area calling, trying to make sense out of the confusion. By the time he was getting close to the entrance to Tory Channel again it was obvious to him that his ship and crew would be needed in a major sea rescue.

Then at last Wellington Radio made contact with his ferry and asked him to proceed to Port Gore and provide whatever help might be needed. It was just as well. He'd more or less decided to go anyway – whatever anyone said. He wished he'd done so on the way in.

John Brew made radio contact with John Reedman on the *Tarihiko*, which by then was trying to find the stricken cruise ship. Apparently she was blacked out and without power.

Because of what seemed a ludicrous and quite unacceptable delay, John Brew was faced with additional problems, matters which could have been avoided. If he had been there more than two hours ago, at least there would have been sufficient light and clear weather to see what was going on.

Darkness was going to make the rescue operation more difficult, and he knew there could be some risk to his own ferry in this uncertain situation.

As he summarised the situation to himself, planning ahead as well as he could in the continuing absence of all the facts, he didn't like the way things were developing – not one bit. It was getting dark, he was an hour or more away from the scene, and radio transmissions seemed to have stopped.

As for the passengers aboard the *Arahura*, they were mostly shocked into silence by the captain's announcement that they were going to divert from their usual course, and why. Local people who had just boarded the ferry were particularly staggered to hear what had apparently happened, and incredulous that it could occur in a place like the Sounds.

Faye Dickson of Whatamango Bay, Picton, was working in Wellington but going home at the weekends. Now she and her son Hamish were returning to work and school respectively. They had seen the *Mikhail Lermontov* during the afternoon. For such a big ship to be in any sort of trouble was something hard to credit. Now they joined other passengers who were questioning and speculating.

At Cape Jackson, Tony and Betty Baker were at their posts in their tiny radio station, and there was nothing a third person could do there.

David Baker decided this was the time for him to give what help he could at the scene, but his fishing launch was out of action. He and his cousin, Denis Cox, got a 14-foot alloy dinghy and outboard motor ready. Some dry clothes and a few apples and biscuits went into a bag in case they were late back.

Prominent fisherman Dave Fishburn, in his fishing charter

launch *Nimrod*, was already on his way, and agreed to call at the Baker jetty to pick the cousins up. He arrived as the intermittent rain started again and the cold wind swung a few more degrees to the south. They talked among themselves of what the rain and cold would do to the elderly passengers on the cruise ship, if things went wrong.

It took all their combined strength to haul the dinghy on to the stern of the *Nimrod*, providing them with a moment of comedy as they faced the possibility of having their own dunking. Then they set off for the cape.

Behind them, dimly through the growing darkness, they could see the *Arahura*, her huge bow wave pounding along behind her. The sight of the ferry under full speed and off her regular course underlined the urgency of the mission. This was a really serious operation. They went out around the lighthouse, thumping through the southerly swell, showering spray high above the launch's wheelhouse, and entered Port Gore. It was around 9pm. The bay looked to be in total darkness. Then a few tiny lights were located.

Using radar navigation, the *Nimrod* and the other small craft which had already gathered felt their way carefully in, looking for the ship they had come to help. The *Tarihiko* and the cement-carrying ship *Golden Bay* had arrived just before them, but neither was equipped with the powerful searchlights which were now badly needed.

Two Havelock-based fishing boats were already in the bay, having intended to shelter there for the night. Mike Harris on *Gypsy*, and Colin McCauley on *Tequila*, had watched in amazement when the Russian ship changed course and headed through the passage. Minutes later they knew she was in trouble. They lifted their anchors and began shadowing the crippled ship.

Mike Harris made radio contact with Don Jamison aboard the *Mikhail Lermontov*, discussing the safest place to run the ship aground. While he spoke he remembered there was a camera on board somewhere, and started rummaging about for it. He took some of the very few photographs of the *Mikhail Lermontov's* last hours.

CHAPTER SIX
Terror in the Darkness

THE *ARAHURA* was manoeuvred to a position about a mile from the stricken vessel, a safe place from which to conduct operations. The bay was completely dark with driving rain and wind gusts to 30 knots.

Captain Brew decided it was time to illuminate the scene. All the deck lights were turned on, including the two powerful searchlights.

Instantly he saw the tiny blips on the radar screens materialise into real life objects. The water was cluttered with rafts, lifeboats, flotsam and jetsam and a number of small rescue craft. The scene was dominated by what he later recalled as the ghost spectre of the crippled liner – starkly white against the blackness of the night. She was listing heavily to starboard, and down by the head. At this moment the enormity of the situation struck all of them on the bridge. None of them had experienced anything like it. At last the problems were real. They galvanised the *Arahura* crew into action.

Captain Brew saw he could do nothing for the *Mikhail Lermontov* herself. The over-riding concern now was maintaining the safety of his own ship with all aboard her, while doing his utmost to bring about the rescue of everyone from the liner. The dangers of collision among all the small craft were also only too apparent.

To the *Arahura's* third officer, Tony Glassey, he gave the task of maintaining the ferry in position. He had to concentrate solely on this, hour after hour, stopping the *Arahura* from drifting and keeping her head to the strengthening southerly wind, using the engines and bow thrusters. The ferry was high in the water and hard to hold steady. There were also risks in anchoring.

This was Tony Glassey's main task that night, but it was a vital job. It enabled Captain Brew to concentrate on the rescue scene, knowing the *Arahura* was safely positioned.

The *Arahura's* passengers and those of the crew who could be spared from duty found the best lookout places they could. Local people tended to cluster together and air their incredulity. In little Picton, nearly everyone knew nearly everyone else. Faye Dickson met up with Don Jamison's son, looking very distressed and concerned about where his father was and any possible involvement he might have in what obviously was a disaster. Faye was forthright in reassuring him. "We know your father. How could he have anything to do with this?"

She and her own son went to the music room so they could see better. From there the cruise ship appeared to be on a beach, or very near it, and it was listing badly.

Over on the *Tarihiko* Captain John Reedman had some heart-stopping moments. A covered lifeboat, with smoke pouring out of its hatch, pulled alongside and a Russian crewman tied it to his tanker. There was enough gas on board the *Tarihiko* to blow them all out of the water. The very last thing he wanted was a burning lifeboat alongside.

A quick inspection showed the smoke was coming from the lifeboat's exhaust pipe, which had broken away and was pumping fumes into the boat, almost suffocating the miserable shipwreck survivors huddled inside.

The *Arahura's* searchlights revealed total confusion. As the ship with the largest rescue capacity, the *Arahura* took over the co-ordinating role at the scene. Captain Brew began organising the rescue craft. He asked the just-arriving cement ship *Milburn Carrier* to stand further off to act as a clearing station for radio messages from Wellington Radio and other shore stations.

Inside Gore Bay, in spite of everything Tony and Betty Baker were doing relaying messages in their little radio station, transmissions were hindered by the high surrounding hills.

John Brew ordered his own lifeboats to be lowered to the water, to be used as lifts to hoist the *Mikhail Lermontov's* passengers aboard.

It was at this stage, as the passengers began to be transferred, that he became aware of just how professional the Russian seamen were. They were soaked to the skin and close to exhaustion from lifting elderly people, but they didn't want to come aboard his ferry. They said they wanted to return to the sinking ship and search for anyone still aboard. Some had to be ordered by their own officers to get aboard the *Arahura*.

Aboard the first lifeboat to reach the *Arahura* were Noeline Rodger and Audrey Peterson, but they had been out in the cold, wet dark for a long time.

They had been in the Bolshoi Lounge when one of its two large steel doors suddenly and loudly banged shut. That was enough to make Noeline and Audrey decide to get out. By now the ship was listing considerably. They milled about with other passengers until someone said they should go down to H deck. There was no panic at all.

"Believe me, Russians are absolute masters at stopping panic," Noeline Rodger said later. "They'd even thrown tarpaulins over the water swirling at the bottom of the stairs, so we wouldn't get frightened."

If anyone had panicked and pushed or shoved, she knew she could have gone down and dislocated her hip or gone into the water. Nobody did.

Once down on H deck they found it level with the water, and a lifeboat alongside. By now it was dark and very wet and cold. After her hip operation, Noeline Rodger couldn't jump. "Come on us, come on us," said one of the Russian crew. "And those big strong seamen with their strong arms just picked us up and carried us into the lifeboat."

The open boat had some blankets but not enough. Noeline saw "only one bit of selfishness". A passenger in a suit had a big Russian blanket which he wouldn't share with anyone, "even the women in sleeveless frocks. That was really terrible."

Next to her was a small woman of about 90. She had been down in the bowels of the ship when a stewardess rushed in, wrapped her in a coat, took her up and carried her into the lifeboat. By now she was really distraught. She had nothing with her, not even her rings, and was beginning to get very upset indeed.

Noeline Rodger knew she must calm her down before she affected others. She said to her the first thing that came into head: "Now listen, dear. All will be well. All your things will be in the customs shed." She said later that she didn't really think she was telling a lie. At that stage she still couldn't believe that the ship would go down. Somehow the authorities would pack up everyone's belongings and somehow everyone would get their things back, she thought.

Her layman's psychology worked, and the older woman became quiet. But when they had rowed near the shore there was no sign of light or life. They sat and shivered and waited.

Then the Russian in charge of the lifeboat said he thought they should sing. They began with Waltzing Matilda, raggedly in the darkness. The 90-year-old who had been on the verge of breaking down started up with It's a Long Way to Tipperary. After that they all just sat until a few people began singing God Save the Queen.

At that point an Australian voice in the darkness called out, "The Queen's all right! Get Him to save *us*."

The Russian in charge produced some freshly baked bread and broke it up. As he gave some to Noeline Rodger he said, "Like Jesus Christ." She realised then that there were a lot of Orthodox Russians among the crew.

As they waited she was seriously alarmed about what would happen if the crew decided to put the passengers ashore. It was cold enough in the lifeboat but if they had to get out and wade or swim through the bitterly cold water, with little warm clothing, and then sit and wait on the shore, she was certain some would die of hypothermia.

At last along came a small fishing trawler, full up with people they'd rescued. The skipper and the Russian conferred. Then Noeline heard "the most wonderful New Zealand voice I've ever heard in my life".

She described it later. "The voice said, 'Yous can just stay in that boat!' I said to him, 'And what are yous gonna do with us?' He said, 'Yous goin to the Picton ferry.'

"I couldn't believe that because there was no sign of anything at all, but suddenly out of the pitch darkness the lights of the ferry came. She looked absolutely huge and absolutely wonderful."

The fishing boat towed them to the *Arahura's* lifeboat which was being winched down. The business of being transferred from one lifeboat to another was terrifying. The water was so choppy everyone was afraid to let go, yet they knew they had to. With one hand Noeline was hanging on to the little old lady she had befriended, and pushed her out first towards the waiting ferry crew who kept shouting to them all to keep their hands out of the way or they would be crushed between the two lifeboats.

"The Russians were absolutely marvellous. They'd risked their lives to save us, and they made no attempt to come with us and be safe on the ferry. They wanted to go and look for other passengers."

From the saloon Faye and Hamish Dickson watched lifeboats full of cold and frightened people, some obviously in pain and in shock, being hoisted up the side of the ferry. Among them were Eric and Phyl Wilkes from Picton who told them the liner's passengers hadn't been informed for a long time about how serious the situation was. But Eric had seen water rushing in, and realised what was going to happen. They had then retrieved their valuables from their cabin, but had lost everything else.

They also told Faye they thought passengers could have been got off earlier if the captain had notified the listening world of the need for early assistance in a very serious situation.

The naval patrol craft, *HMNZS Taupo*, and the police launch, *Lady Elizabeth II*, had arrived. They joined in the search for possible survivors in the water. Watching closely, Captain Brew was concerned by *Taupo's* speed as she nosed about among the debris. The ship seemed to be almost unmanagable if taken below eight knots. This meant there was a risk that anyone in the water would be run over.

Then his eye suddenly caught something gleaming in the searchlight beam. The light tracked back, to find the glint of reflector tape on a lifejacket worn by a passenger in the water. Captain Brew directed *Taupo* to pick him up; the man became the only passenger to enjoy the hospitality of the Navy that momentous night. All the others were eventually taken on board by the *Arahura* and the *Tarihiko*. The Russian crew members manning the lifeboats were attracted like moths to the blaze of their lights. The tiny craft swarmed towards them.

It had been dark by the time David Baker and Denis Cox could launch their dinghy from the stern of the *Nimrod*. The bay seemed full of boats of all sizes, and they had no doubts about the dangerous situation they were entering. Both were experienced small boat skippers who knew how quickly accidents could happen, specially with lots of small craft operating close together in the darkness. "We'd better be bloody careful here, or we could be run down," David said.

As they got alongside the cruise ship they could see that the huge port side propeller was well clear of the water. Several fishing boats were taking off passengers. Lifeboats, and rafts full of people, seemed to be floating aimlessly in the darkness with no-one in charge.

The slight sea chop which had developed when the wind changed was no problem for the 14-foot open boat, but the wakes rebounding off the hull of the sinking ship were creating a hazard. One of the wakes belonged to the *Arahura*, but despite the hazard of her wake, the men were glad to see her. Nevertheless, "This is too bloody dangerous for us," David Baker decided. "We'd better get over by the ferry and pick up anyone who falls overboard. The bigger boats will have the job under control."

Denis agreed. They started to motor over to the ferry, which was beginning to lower her lifeboats over the side to collect passengers. Away off beyond the *Arahura* they caught a glimpse of a liferaft full of people, which seemed not to be under power. They went to check. Their alloy dinghy got there quickly, to find it was full of Russian crew. Without waiting for discussion they took the bow line, tied it to the stern of their dinghy, then set off back towards the *Arahura* with the heavy liferaft in tow.

From a fishing boat a man shouted, "There's someone in a lifejacket in the water, over there by the ship!" As they were close the ferry they dropped the tow line and went racing to the indicated spot, near the bow, frantically peering into the dark water. They searched along the starboard side of the ship which was slowly sinking lower towards the water. They couldn't see anybody, but found an apparently empty liferaft trapped under the stern of the ship.

The beams from their hand-held spotlights appeared to be swallowed up in the darkness. They shouted, but got no response. To venture under the stern and propellers of the ship, which were well clear of the water, would be extremely risky. After calling a few more times and getting no response they reluctantly backed off, with a sickening feeling that there could have been some elderly frightened people under there waiting to be rescued, but whom they had been unable to help.

A sense of frustration and helplessness swept over them. They hadn't been able to help get passengers off the ship, and they'd possibly missed someone in the water, abandoning them trapped under the sinking ship, with little chance of survival.

They were heading back to the *Nimrod* to ask for instructions or suggestions when they saw a Navy patrol craft appear out of the darkness, coming so close to the launch that Dave Fishburn had to throw his engine astern to avoid a collision.

David and Denis could see other lifejackets floating on the surface in the rain, but all were empty, and they had no way of knowing if they had been worn by someone who had perished, or whether they'd been thrown away. Inflatable liferafts also appeared out of the darkness, and had to be checked for survivors.

All around seemed to be chaos and confusion, and they chugged about checking and re-checking empty liferafts. They began helping take some to the beach, as they were hindering the search, but the large inflatable raft they'd taken in tow was slow to haul behind their dinghy. A loud-hailer message from the Navy boat instructed that anything that could not be towed was to be sunk. David produced a fishing knife. A few stabs, and the inflatable raft collapsed with a loud hiss, to disappear beneath the water.

Aboard the *Fugitive*, the Heberleys arrived to find the bay a mass of lights. The ferry's powerful searchlights blinded them when they turned in their direction. The cruise ship still had her own lights at that time, and Joe Heberley was amazed to see what the passengers were wearing. "There they were, being lifted down into lifeboats, and they weren't dressed for a shipwreck at all. Most were wearing flimsy evening dress."

Those whose evening gowns were topped off by fur coats may have fared better. Later, however, when Joe and his sons were asked to take empty lifeboats in tow for Picton, they saw, lying abandoned in the bottom of one boat, "the most beautiful fur coat". They touched nothing, and the fur lay there for the long tow to Picton.

But for the present the main concern was locating all the lifeboats that were drifting out of the bay, to see if any contained people. The Navy boat asked them to take over this job. The motorised Russian boats had been towing others to the *Tarihiko* and *Arahura*, and, once people were transferred to safety, these lifeboats were simply let go. Nobody knew whether survivors were in these boats or on rafts, or not. In the dark drizzly rain, they were just blips on the radar.

"It was bedlam. Just bedlam. The motorised Russian lifeboats, which were capable of up to twenty knots, were charging around, and the sea seemed covered with boats and rafts."

The Heberleys also stabbed inflatable rafts, and investigated floating lifejackets which stood out because of their strips of reflector tapes. Larger, solidly built boats were difficult to tow as they were about 20 metres long and had no towing points.

Every time they looked at the sinking ship, the crowds of passengers waiting to be taken off seemed to grow no smaller.

Then the *Fugitive* was given the job of taking command of a motorised boat that seemed to be going nowhere. They came up alongside it, and a Russian crewman asked Joe, "Where's Picton?" It wasn't the time to engage in conversation, and Joe simply directed them towards one of the rescue ships.

If the *Arahura* and *Tarihiko* hadn't been there, Joe wondered, whatever would have become of all the lifeboats? It was dark, there was an offshore wind, and they were in "pretty rugged country".

Lifeboats and fishing boats still lined up at the embarkation doors to take loads of mostly traumatised passengers out to the tanker or ferry, while the *Mikhail Lermontov* moved slowly through gathering darkness and on the rising tide towards the beach. The rain became heavier, to add to everyone's misery.

Separate dramas were still being played out aboard the cruise ship. As the minutes ticked by, the picture of the ship being sucked inexorably under, taking them all with her, kept rushing into everyone's mind.

Earlier, when the list had increased to an alarming 16 degrees, Mark Raymond had had to fight against his fear that the ship would roll over and trap him inside. And there still seemed to be hundreds of passengers waiting to be helped.

An Australian woman asked him to get as many blankets from the cabins as he could, at the same time making sure no one was left behind. He grabbed armsful of blankets and threw them into the lifeboats waiting below.

People huddled in their blankets, although not everyone had even that comfort, holding whatever personal belongings they had managed to grab.

One weeping woman clutched her hairbrush. It was all she had apart from the nightclothes she was wearing.

From her vantage point Julie Smith had watched the lifeboats being swung over the *Mihail Lermontov's* side. That part happened very quickly, but then came a long period of waiting in queues. They were told the boats would be landing on the shore, which Julie thought was strange as she knew this shore had no road access.

Three times in all, Julie along with Julie Dalmazzo lined up for a lifeboat, only to be told twice that they were full. They then had to go up or down stairs and along corridors to queue for another boat.

The two friends were helping the 'oldies', as Julie Smith thought of them, and getting frustrated when one woman objected to being hastened along. They decided there could come a time when they just had to look after themselves, fast, which might mean jumping over the side. Both women were good swimmers, and not afraid of being in the water, but they didn't want to create any panic by taking their own course of action.

When they finally got to board a lifeboat, the deck was listing so badly they began slipping. A crewman passed a rope down the queue so people could approach the disembarking point. Once there, they had the rope ladder to contend with. Another crew member held onto Julie's arms until she got her footing and kept hold until Julie could support herself. At the end of the ladder she practically had to jump onto the shoulders of another crewman. As she was passed into the lifeboat, Julie was grateful for what seemed to be the incredible strength of the crewmen – and she observed how much lighter she was than many others they'd caught.

It was a covered-in boat, and this was Julie's undoing. She suffered a panic attack, and began to gasp for breath. Someone lent her their Ventolin spray, and took her lifejacket off, and she managed to hold herself together while their boat motored around and took some of the open, oars-only, boats in tow.

The more elderly passengers still on board the cruise ship were having trouble getting into the lifeboats. Progress slowed, and tension levels rose. The last thing that was needed was panic among the passengers. But the crew had to speed up the disembarkation; Captain Vorobyov asked for a lifeboat to be sent from the *Tarihiko* to assist.

Things went all right until the bow line from one of the ship's lifeboats got tangled in the *Tarihiko* lifeboat's propeller.

Then there was nothing for it but to transfer people from one to the other, a painfully slow process.

The list increased to 18 degrees. The situation was critical. A quick survey showed there were still at least 80 passengers on board.

Joan Dillon and her daughter Gail Cottle had been mighty relieved when the announcement had finally come that they were to go to the lifeboats. They'd waited anxiously for several hours, not knowing what was happening, so they headed eagerly for their lifeboat station.

Outside on deck they both became soaked by the rain but they hurried along with the others. When they reached their appointed station there was no-one in charge to tell them what to do. They stood anxiously in the cold rain while the ship's list worsened.

Eventually a Russian woman crew member came and indicated they were all to follow her to another lifeboat station. They went through the interior of the ship to a narrow corridor, then on to a staircase with a steel door at the top. It obviously led to the outside, but was firmly shut. The ship was now listing over so far that people were slipping and falling down the stairs. On one side a wooden rail provided a hand-hold, and they clung to that.

The woman rushed off to attend to other duties, saying there would be someone to help them "in a short time".

Here they were crammed together in the near-dark, in a crowded, frightened, part-vertical queue. No-one knew what was happening.

After what seemed an eternity, other Russian crew members arrived to tie a rope from the steel door to the bottom of the stairwell for people to hang on to. These crew members, too, left as quickly as they had arrived.

Now began the worst nightmare of all. The passengers couldn't go back. Water was now swirling in below. They couldn't go forward. The steel door blocked their way. They had to wait in their dark prison, in what they now all knew to be a sinking ship.

They estimate they were left for an hour and a half. They didn't know where in the ship they were. Worse, they didn't know if anybody in authority knew where they were.

Joan Dillon, resolute woman though she was, became seriously distressed by the growing black-out and the oppressive warmth of the crowded staircase. There seemed no movement of the air, as if they might suffocate. Her arms and neck burned with the strain of holding on to the rope to support herself.

Behind her an elderly woman sounded as if she were having a heart attack. Trying to comfort her, Joan wondered if she would have the strength to hold on to both the rope and the other woman if she collapsed.

She was convinced they had been forgotten. They would be trapped when the ship went down. Guilt assailed her. Why on earth had she brought her daughter with her on this terrible voyage? Gail had a husband and family back in Australia. How would Gail's family be able to cope without her?

Voices rose and fell as people encouraged one another or asked others to move a little and make room in the packed stairwell. Sudden cries kept erupting against a background of quiet weeping or praying.

Someone cursed the "stupid bloody Russians" for running the ship aground, and others joined in. Yet others blamed themselves for even being on the ship.

One old man was almost hysterical because he couldn't find his wife. She was nearly blind, he said, and they'd got separated in the Bolshoi Lounge. He kept saying he wanted to get out and find her but he couldn't get out of the stairwell. Others tried to calm him but he seemed not to hear them.

Tom Archer was near the top of the stairs. He was hanging on to the wooden rail with one hand, with his other arm around his wife to support her, when a man above them lost his footing and came tumbling down. He crashed into several people, sending Dorothy Archer backwards down the steep stairwell. When her frantic husband managed to push and shove his way down to reach her, she was lying quite still, blood oozing from a cut on her forehead.

The water at the bottom of the stairwell was mere inches from her feet. When she opened her eyes Tom told her to roll on to her front, so he could help her to her feet, but the floor was at too steep a pitch for them. She began to panic. To calm her Tom said the first thing that came into his mind. "Don't worry – we can both swim, and there's plenty of furniture floating about to hang on to."

At last the door above them opened and a Russian crewman appeared with a rope, which he lowered. People began to haul themselves up, slowly and clumsily, groaning and panting, past others who were falling down.

Somewhere in the darkness someone was praying.

Many passengers who had managed to get to the main embarkation door or the stern had to be physically carried onto the motor tenders which had transferred their first loads of passengers, and returned for more. Among them was Sheila Simpson, who, like many others, froze when her turn came to climb down a rope ladder against the side of the ship.

The dark, the looming sea and the windblown rain made it a truly horrifying prospect. "I can't, I can't!" Sheila Simpson called out, but the Russian crewman said, "Go, lady, go, more people behind you." Still she could not move. A crewman deftly tied a rope around her chest under her arms, and lowered her, screaming, into the darkness. One of the crew of a fishing boat caught her.

Tom Archer was determined to climb down the rope ladder unaided. He was making good progress until, unexpectedly, the ladder ran out about six feet too soon. He was suspended in the darkness. A voice somewhere below called, "Let go! We will catch you!"

There was nothing else for it. He let go, dropping about six feet into the waiting arms of a fisherman. In the boat his wife was safe and sound, but Sheila, his sister-in-law, was in agony with a suspected broken leg. The fishing boat, now full of passengers, headed for the *Arahura*.

The *Mikhail Lermontov's* list had increased to nearly 28

degrees, making it difficult for anyone to keep their footing. Yet the people in the stairwell still had to pull themselves up, using the rope. Next they had to turn around backwards at the steel door, then climb down a rope ladder against the side of the ship. Just as she at last reached the top, Joan Dillon lost her footing and fell heavily. She held grimly on to the rope with one hand, knowing that, if she let it go, she mightn't be able to get back up the sloping deck again in the darkness.

She and Gail were close to complete exhaustion after their long and terrifying ordeal in the darkened stairwell. Through it all, Joan Dillon had managed to keep her handbag on one shoulder and their travel bag on the other. But the Russian crewmen knew they must get the last of the passengers off before the ship rolled over or sank under them, so they grabbed both bags from her and unceremoniously threw them over the side. They missed the lifeboat and fell into the sea. In them were letters and poems written by her late husband. They were precious pages, so precious to her that she had brought them with her for safekeeping rather than leaving them in her Australian home.

With more passengers being pushed and hustled down from above by the increasingly anxious crew, Joan Dillon half fell and half jumped into the waiting lifeboat, landing on her back against the hard edge. She was almost beside herself with fear and pain and distress. The rain continued to pour down on her misery.

But Gail was now in the lifeboat. Joan Dillon tried to concentrate on that thought.

For many of the other passengers who had been trapped in the stairwell, it now seemed an impossible task to leave the liner. They simply had no physical or mental energy left. Crewmen, many also close to exhaustion, lifted people bodily through the door on to the rope ladder, where more froze out of fear. With the rope ladder hard against the sloping side of the ship, finding a foothold was difficult even for able-bodied seamen.

Then, when they finally all got into the lifeboat, the motor failed as it tried to pull away. The crew struggled to get it started again, and someone cried out, "She's going to sink any minute!"

If the ship went down, everyone knew they would be sucked down, too, to go to the bottom with her.

In the darkness an old man, his fear now turned to anger, swore loudly. "If they'd left us in that dark hell-hole another eight minutes we'd be going down with her. We should've been in the lifeboats bloody hours ago!"

Ray and Lorna Leihn and the two boys had clung to each other, and were among the last in their group to go over the side. As the crew began to lower the big lifeboat ready to get the passengers into it, it caught against the side of the listing ship and wouldn't move. The crew decided to get the passengers into the boat to add more weight.

When this didn't work, everyone was instructed to push against the side of the ship. It sounded ridiculous, but they leaned out and pushed. The lifeboat was lowered some six feet before it stuck again, supported by the side of the ship which was leaning the opposite way. More bumping and more pushing freed it. They finally reached the water, wet, exhausted and bruised.

A crewman still on deck threw a couple of cartons into the lifeboat. Ray thought they were emergency rations or first aid supplies. One landed near Lorna's feet. It burst open to reveal a case of vodka. The other parcel was of crew clothing.

On the starboard side of the ship, getting off was a little easier, as the embarkation doors were almost at water level and passengers had only a small distance to step down into the lifeboats. Jean Thorpe, cold in thin white slacks and top, stepped on to the wooden seat and her leg went straight through the rotten timber to the bottom of the alloy boat.

Others had noticed the poor state of the lifejackets, some of which fell apart in their hands, and some complained that, the liner having been built in Germany, instructions on the lifeboats and lifejackets were written in German as well as Russian – but not in English.

Someone had called out, "Women and children first!" Harry Thomas wasn't sure if it was a crewman or one of the passengers, but everyone seemed to be obeying the instruction and he reluctantly helped his wife into a lifeboat and waved bravely to her as it pulled away into the engulfing darkness. He wondered if he would ever see her again.

Soon he was helped into another lifeboat, to find it was half full of people shaking with cold and shock. They had been among the first to leave the ship, nearly two hours earlier, but they had sat unprotected in the rain since then.

In another lifeboat Bunny Gibson was still at work, keeping up her comedy act. One woman was bemoaning the loss of the lovely flowers she'd arranged all around her cabin. Bunny couldn't resist the opening: "Well, you've no need to worry about them getting water, dear, have you?"

A grandmother also had a positive attitude. "I have a grandson," she said, "who has pink punk hair and one earring and who always says, 'Oh come on, Nan, why don't you do anything exciting?' Now I can say, 'I was in a shipwreck the other day.'"

Bunny's boat was adrift for what seemed hours. Though everyone was cold, wet and hungry, there was actually much laughter and singing on board – tears would come later. Flares showed the ship sinking lower and lower.

A larger boat eventually came alongside, but it was already too full to pick them up. They were assured of being taken in tow soon, and before leaving them this boat passed down blankets and bread. The Russians cut the loaves up with their penknives, and passed them out. Bunny, falling back on her 'Rita-the-ETA-Eater' routine in television commercials for margarine, apologised for not being able to provide the real thing. Someone should dive down to catch fish, she said, so at least they could have loaves and fishes.

On the top deck Lorand Loblay was translating for the Russian crew members who were loading people into the lifeboats. Passengers were milling around because their pre-allocated stations were no longer available. The boats had been half-lowered to be filled from H deck, but were now being boarded from one deck higher because of the increasing list of the ship. Because of this, the rope ladders guiding people down the *Lermontov's* hull were too short by about two metres. Passengers, climbing down, had to nerve themselves to let go of the rope ladder, and trust they would be caught by those already in the boat.

Lorand said goodbye to his companion, entrusting her to the care of a crew member. He gave assistance to passengers near the bow, translating for a crewman who kept repeating, "Women and children first!" Some male passengers stood aside, but others ignored the call, and reached for the rope ladder. In the rain and darkness, loading the boats seemed to take an eternity, but finally only a handful of passengers were left.

Lorand heard a cry come down in Russian, "Let's take to the boats!" and the crewman he was helping pushed him towards the rope ladder. Lorand hung his legs over the railing, got hold of the rope, swung himself out, and let go when he'd descended as far as the rope would allow.

The remaining crew on deck began to work the winch to lower the boat. It hit the side of the ship with a great lurch, but no-one fell out. Crew members pushed with oars to stop the lifeboat hitting again, but it repeatedly swung against the hull.

When they finally hit the water, Lorand was concerned that the ship might sink before they got a safe distance away. The motor of his lifeboat – as was the case with many of them – didn't work, so the crew started rowing furiously. To raise spirits, Lorand began singing old Russian folk songs, and soon crew members joined in.

From the sloping bridge Captain Vorobyov could see that the last of the passengers would soon be taken off. It was now time to get his crew to safety. The engine room crew in particular were in danger if they remained below. They had stuck bravely to their tasks in frightening conditions, literally with water underfoot. Now, with all power lost, there was no reason for them to remain. He ordered them to leave their stations.

The ship by now had a 20-degree list to starboard. Captain Vorobyov ordered the remaining crew to abandon ship.

An easterly wind had pushed the helpless vessel along the sand bar for a while, but the wind swung to the south and strengthened, and she was drifting back into deep water towards Gannet Point. Captain Vorobyov asked Don Jamison to call the *Tarihiko* and ask Captain Reedman to use his ship to push the *Mikhail Lermontov* closer to the shore.

"I can't do that," Captain Reedman replied. "My ship isn't gas-free, and I have survivors on board."

The *Tarihiko* had a cargo capacity of 1,000 tonnes of highly volatile LPG, but even when the ship was supposedly empty, there was a residual 30 tonnes of the explosive gas in the three deck tanks. A mishap or collision could spark a devastating explosion.

Captain Brew had also considered the possibility of pushing the ship ashore, to prevent it from sinking, but had soon discounted the idea. The bulbous bow of the *Arahura* might be seriously damaged. He decided it could not be done. If only, he thought, he had arrived there in daylight. Then it could have been a different story.

Captain Vorobyov had not given up completely. With luck his ship still might run aground in water shallow enough for her to be salvagable. A seaman had just reported that there were 21 metres of water under the bow, and 43 metres under the stern. That was far too deep. If she settled on the bottom in that depth of water she would never be lifted again.

But there was still a chance she would run aground in shallow water off Gannet Point. It was going to be an exacting and difficult thing to get right; if they let the anchors go too soon, that would be the end of the ship. They had no power to lift the anchors once they were out.

On the bridge of the *Tarihiko*, Captain Reedman was using his radar to keep track of events. He saw that the *Mikhail Lermontov* had started to move again, directly towards his anchored ship. He turned to his navigator and asked, "Will she hit us on that course?"

"I think she will, John. We'd better get the anchors aboard and get out of the way."

Captain Reedman called to first mate Rod Theobold to get the anchors up and prepare to move. Then things began to go wrong.

"Skipper, we've got a lifeboat tied alongside!" one of his crew called out. "I didn't see it arrive but it's got about a hundred old people – and they want to come aboard."

As the skipper was considering how to handle that situation, the first mate called to say the port anchor chain had jammed. He couldn't get the anchor aboard.

The anchor chain fault was a familiar problem. Instead of falling evenly to the bottom of its locker as it came aboard, the heavy chain would sometimes form a mound and block the entrance. The solution was to let the anchor drop to the seafloor, then lift it again.

They tried this. It jammed again. They tried a second time, everyone intent on the procedure while Captain Reedman watched the looming white liner drift towards his helpless ship. Again the anchor chain jammed. On the third by now desperate attempt, the anchor finally came aboard and the *Tarihiko* moved slowly ahead, the lifeboat still tied alongside. A mere hundred metres away, the crippled *Mikhail Lermontov* slipped slowly and eerily past the stern.

With this crisis past, Captain Reedman could at last put his port lifeboat over the side to help evacuate passengers from the Russian lifeboat, and his crew began helping people aboard from the tethered boat.

On the cruise ship, crew members were helping the last passengers into the ship's two motor tenders. Others of the crew were by now scrambling down embarkation ladders into lifeboats. They set out to row through the teeming rain to the

The cruise ship *Mikhail Lermontov*. In less than 16 hours from when this picture was taken on 16 February 1986, she was at the bottom of the sea.

Russian folk dancing in the Bolshoi Lounge was always popular with cruise passengers.

'Captain's Cocktail Night' aboard the *Mikhail Lermontov*. Russian officers back their captain in the Bolshoi Lounge. In this photo the captain, with the microphone, is Captain Oram Organov. When the tragedy occurred, he was waiting in Sydney to rejoin his ship, and take over from Captain Vladislav Vorobyov.

Photo C.T.C.

Some of the ship's entertainment team and Russian diningroom staff ready for 'Island Night'.

Photo Jean Anderson

Left: Captain Vladislav Vorobyov back at sea again. Photo taken a decade after the loss of the *Mikhail Lermontov*. Right: Captain Don Jamison.

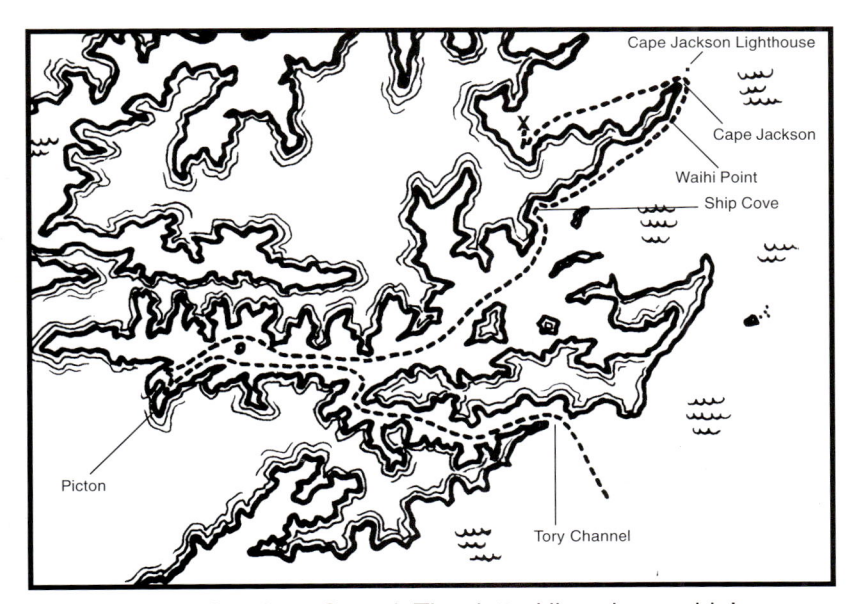

Map of Queen Charlotte Sound. The dotted line shows ship's course.

This reconstruction shows the *Mikhail Lermontov* in relation to Cape Jackson and Jackson Head, at approximately her position when she grounded. Below: The seafloor illustration comes from chart data from 1895 – the only official survey of the passage. It is believed that the ship struck Perham Rock.

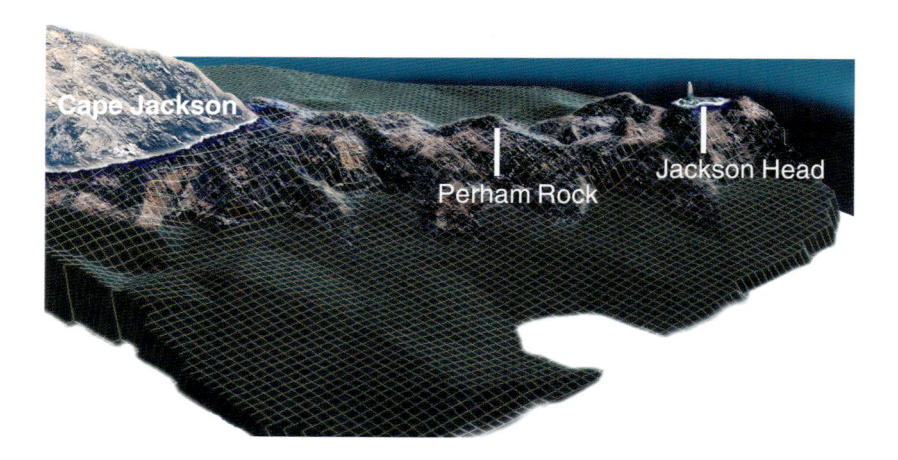

Wireframe rendering from Hydrographic Office, RNZN. (Topography is approximate, based on available soundings).

The announcement, "Dinner will be late" gave passengers Mavis, Heather, Dell and Harry the cue to put on their life jackets. Dinner was never served.

Diagram of the *Mikhail Lermontov* showing large gashes in the port side below the waterline, and 100ft aft of the bow thruster port.

Light fades as the Russian captain searches for somewhere to beach his ship in Port Gore.

Photos Mike Harris

Photo Mike Harris

Local fishing boats gather to help rescue the cruise ship's passengers and crew.

Photo David Trigg

Death of a cruise ship. The *Mikhail Lermontov* slips beneath the waters of Port Gore.

Left: Captain John Brew, master of the *Arahura* on the fateful night.
Right: Captain John Reedman, master of the *Tarihiko*.

Ray and Lorna Leihn and their grandsons Steven, six, (left), and John, eight, are welcomed on board the *Arahura* by steward Brian Harmon. The Leihns, in one of the last lifeboats, were rowed to safety by Russian seamen.

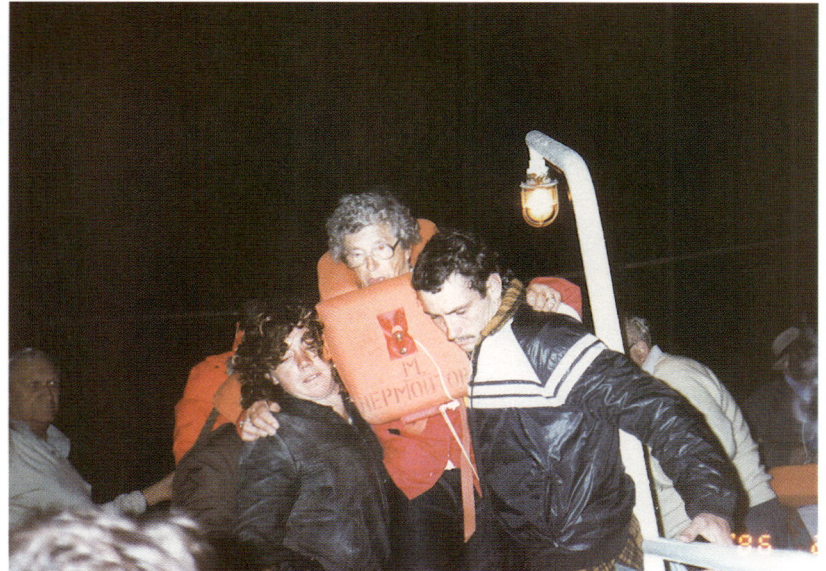

Few were dressed for a shipwreck. Passengers, wet, cold and exhausted, are transferred from the cruise ship's lifeboats to those of the *Arahura*, then hauled up to the deck and helped aboard the ferry.

Somebody's handbag, somebody's emergency blanket – most passengers had to abandon ship with no more than they were wearing for an evening of fun and dancing.

Betty Baker at the controls of Port Jackson Radio. She and her husband Tony served as the vital centre of the rescue co-ordination.

Photos Ray O'Neill

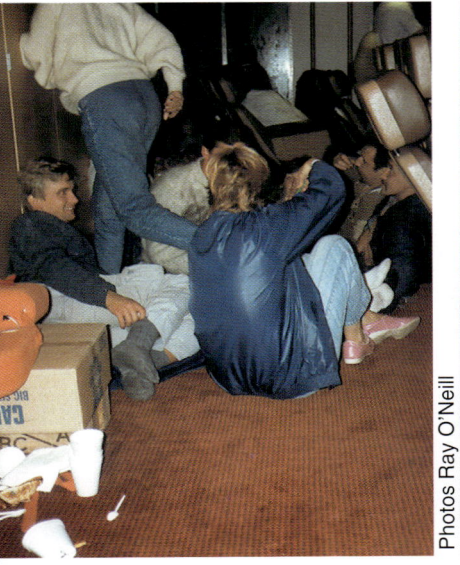

Left: Stretched out or huddled where they could, shipwrecked passengers on their way to Wellington aboard the *Arahura*. Right: Life jackets, their purpose at an end.

The two Julies, Julie Smith (left) and Julie Read.

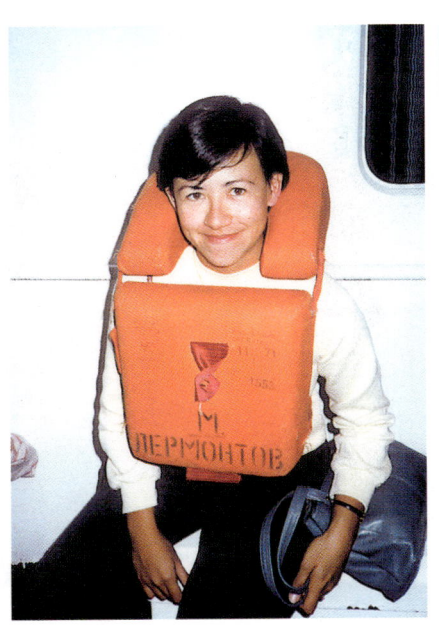

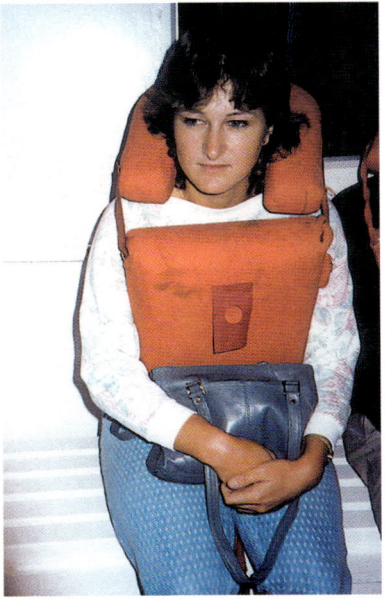

Photos Julie Read

The Heberley fishing boat, the *Fugitive*, towed empty lifeboats to Picton

Captain Steve Ponsford who conducted the enquiry into the loss of the *Mikhail Lermontov*

Entertainment staff (from left) Lee Young, Jean Anderson, Bunny Gibson, here at 'Island Night", kept up passengers' morale in the lifeboats.

Photo Jean Anderson

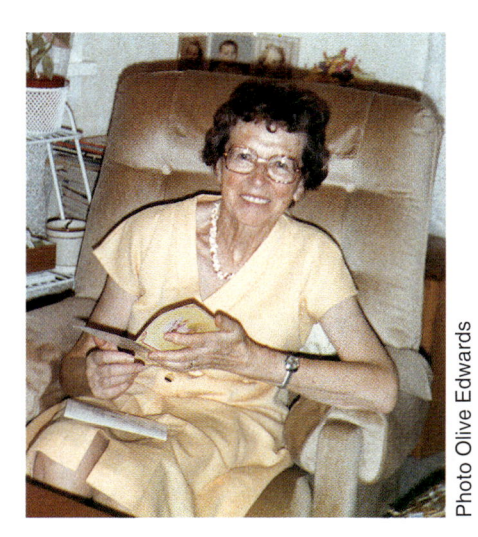

Photo Olive Edwards

Passenger Olive Edwards insisted on a longer holiday.

Photo Lorand Loblay

Lorand Loblay, the passenger best placed to know what was going on.

The salvage team brings up the ship's bell, Ray Hatch (left) and Doug Taylor.

Photo Ray Harris

Up from the bottom of the sea – shore excursion officer Jean Anderson with her pearls, now black, which were salvaged from her cabin.

Photo Ray Hatch

Souvenir coins salvaged by recreation diver Jeremy Brew.

Photo Jeremy Brew

Captain Vladislav Vorobyov (second from left) is flanked by Soviet officials as he arrives to give evidence at the enquiry.

Key figure in the Marlborough Harbour Board's political turmoil, general manager Mike Goulden.

Chairman of the Marlborough Harbour Board when the cruise ship sank, Bruno Dalliessi.

Marlborough Harbour Board, December 1985. Back row: N. R. Johnson, R. G. Taylor *(Harbour Engineer)*, G. B. Riach *(Operations Manager)*, E. L. Collins, E. Chaney *(Treasurer)*. Middle row: J. J. Webb, J. Woodhall, A. R. Kennington, A. D. Cambridge, L. W. Williams, J. R. Abernethy. Front row: I. G. Nicol *(Secretary)*, G. S. Fuller, B. J. Dalliessi *(Chairman)*, G. H. Robb, D. I. Jamison *(Harbourmaster & Acting General Manager)*, T. S. Eckford.

Tarihiko, which was filling with exhausted passengers.

By now the ship's list had increased to about 25 degrees. She could go at any time. The captain had done all he could to save his ship. Now she was at the mercy of the wind and the sea.

CHAPTER SEVEN

Death Throes of a Ship

CAPTAIN BREW had brought the *Arahura* as close as he dared, and was taking the last of the passengers and crew from the lifeboats. Of the *Mikhail Lermontov's* crew there were only the captain, the senior officers and Captain Jamison left on the bridge.

The last of the passengers were in a lifeboat beside the ship. Captain Vorobyov ordered everyone to follow them, except for the chief navigator, the purser and the watch officer who would wait with him on his dying ship. Each of these men had packets of ship's documents and passports to carry to safety. He ordered chief navigator Sergey Stepanishchev and second officer Sergey Gusev to the main embarkation door. He himself went with purser Aleksey Zhivotenkov to the door at the stern.

He still had the terrible feeling there could be someone left on board. He took the lifeboat mooring lines from the last two sailors, and spoke to them quietly. They were young and fit, but shaking with exhaustion after lifting dozens of people into the motor tenders. Were they sure there was no-one left on board? Yes, they were sure. Would they make a last quick check of all the corridors?

The two seamen glanced at each other for a second. Then, obediently, they disappeared into the pitch-dark ship. If she rolled, they would go down with her.

Captain Vorobyov waited for them to return, holding on to the last lifeboat. After an eternity, a matter of minutes, they came back to report calmly that there was no-one left on board.

Many passengers would later claim they were the last, or among the last, to leave the *Mikhail Lermontov*. Lorand Loblay believed his boat was among the last, but attached no great importance to the fact. Claims of being last off could be due to the need some people always seem to have to romanticise or embellish their stories with a touch of heroism.

But there was confusion, it was dark, and visibility was limited. If, while people were boarding a lifeboat, no other could be seen, they could appear to be the last. At times a lowered lifeboat dangled in mid-air for some time, as ropes and winches were dealt with, so that a boat lowered seemingly later might hit the sea first.

Lee Young, busy helping the elderly into lifeboats, found the minutes went quickly, too quickly when the ship seemed on the very verge of sinking and the passengers seemed to move so very slowly. He believed his own disembarkation, along with some officers, crew and a few elderly women, was the last, with their boat hitting the sea at approximately 10.25pm.

As Lorand's boat pulled away, he could see the captain's motor boat, lit up, bobbing beside the ship.

The *Mikhail Lermontov* was now almost lying on her starboard side, with the port bilge keels clear of the water.

The sailors moved to take the mooring line from their captain to let him get into the lifeboat. But he gave them each a firm pat on the shoulder and ordered them off the ship. He would be the last away. Then he jumped to the reaching hands of his crew in the last lifeboat.

As they pulled away there was no doubt that the liner would sink in deep water, and be unsalvagable. The wind had been enough to move her off the sand bar, near Tunnel Bay, but not strong enough to push her ashore at Gannet Point. Her bow was under water. The first letters of her name had disappeared beneath the sea.

On the *Tarihiko* Captain Reedman had new problems to deal with. His port side lifeboat with three of his crew had not returned, and he had lost radio contact with them. The sea all around his ship still seemed littered with lifeboats and small boats, and he couldn't make out his own among them.

Had they been run over by another boat? Or had an accident of some sort? He wasn't going to leave the bay without finding them.

In an oar-powered lifeboat full of Russian-speaking crew and wet, exhausted passengers, Clare Stevenson gathered her thoughts. She had had to stand in the cold rain on a sloping deck with dozens of other passengers, waiting to be told what to do next. At long last they had been led to the side of the ship and told to climb down a rope ladder.

At that point her strength and her courage had almost given out. From an early age she'd ridden her pony alone around her family's paddocks, climbed trees and shinnied up and down ropes as well as any boy. Nobody then had thought of the slogan, "Girls can do anything", but that summed up the way the young Clare Stevenson faced the world.

As a student at the University of Melbourne she had stood out as a leader, too, particularly in matters concerning the status of women. But that was then. Now she was 82 years old and her joints were stiff with cold as well as age.

She had frozen with her hand clenched tightly on the guardrail. Without the help of the Russian crew she would never had made it. At last she'd been handed into the boat. In spite of the fear and confusion all around her she'd thanked each one of the crew as graciously as if they were opening a door for her at home.

Now her arms still hurt from hanging on to the rope ladder and her legs trembled, partly from the strain of climbing down the side of the ship, and partly from relief. She was sore, bruised and cold. It had been terrifying, but already she was thinking what a story she could make of this whole adventure when she addressed her main organisation, the Carers' Association of New South Wales, or one of the many groups of which she was patron. She couldn't help laughing at the thought. But how could she make everyone at home understand what it was like to be in a lifeboat full of foreign sailors and shivering elderly passengers, fleeing from a sinking ship in the dark?

Then she realised they were scarcely moving. The bulk of the *Mikhail Lermontov* loomed uncomfortably close. They had to get away or they would be sucked down when she sank. Yet they were making no progress. The oars crashed against each other, dipping in and out without rhythm. The Russian sailors didn't seem to know about rowing. There was no co-ordination. Nobody was in charge. Everyone was shouting, and nobody was listening.

It was second nature for Clare Stevenson to organise people. Almost all her long life she had been a leader. Russians they might be, and non-English speaking, but they could follow instructions as well as anyone else, as long as they understood what was being said. It never crossed her mind they would ignore her. Nobody ignored Clare Stevenson.

She mentally rehearsed the language lessons the stewardesses had given her. Then, at first shouting to be heard above the moans and cries around her, then loudly and confidently and rhythmically, she began to count.

"*Odeen, dva! Odeen, dva!*" (One, two! One, two!)

Others took up the chant and someone called out, "Come on, Ivan, get your act sorted!" One bearded sailor looked at Clare in astonishment, then grinned hugely and took up the count. More passengers joined in while others cheered the crew on. The unwieldy lifeboat moved away from the doomed ship, the long oars dipping into the dark water now in almost perfect unison.

Captain Vorobyov directed his tender towards the *Arahura*, which had lifeboats swung out on their davits, but not reaching the water. As he got closer he realised they were too high for safe transfer of passengers from his tender. He headed for the *Tarihiko*, which was anchored with all her lights blazing. Part way across he encountered one of the *Mikhail Lermontov's* motor lifeboats full of passengers, huddled in blankets and bright orange lifejackets, others soaked to the skin in the light clothing they had been wearing when the ship struck.

Also in the convoy was the missing *Tarihiko* lifeboat. It had got caught in the press of boats around the sinking ship and had been partially swamped. The hand-held radio had fallen into the water, but everyone on board was safe.

Captain Vorobyov joined the head of the little convoy and helped tow it to the tanker, where ladders had been lowered down the port side.

With the last of the lifeboats secured alongside the *Tarihiko*, the Russian master pulled his tender away to keep an eye on proceedings in case someone fell overboard. At last all were aboard and safe except for the passengers and crew he had with him. He moved alongside the high-sided tanker and prepared to help everyone off the tender and up the ladders. From high above on the *Tarihiko* bridge, an officer called, "We are full to capacity. There's no more room! You'll have to go back to the ferry."

Captain Vorobyov ordered the helmsman to take them back to the *Arahura*, a mile and a half away in the darkness, and sat down to contact his officers on their hand-radio sets. He was still not absolutely sure that all the passengers had been safely taken off his ship, and he was deeply worried about his crew. They had worked bravely and tirelessly, in dangerous conditions, and he wanted to be sure they were all right. Some were on the *Tarihiko*, some on the *Arahura*, and at least one motor tender was still cruising about in the darkness looking for anyone possibly bobbing around in the dark sea.

As the replies came back he was still not sure if people were missing. By this time they had got alongside the *Arahura*. By now her lifeboats had been lowered right to the water. Twenty-five passengers and crew at a time were hoisted aboard, until he was left with seven of his crew. He contacted the tender by radio and ordered the helmsman to continue searching the area, then climbed into the *Arahura's* lifeboat.

Out in the bay Vorobyov could see his ship, stricken, on her side. The way she lay in the water reminded Captain Brew of "a wounded white whale".

The brilliant searchlights, still scanning the water for survivors, lit up the scene every time they swept over the white hull.

"My God, there she goes!" someone suddenly shouted.

There was a great intake of breath. The huge ship started moving faster. She had been sliding slowly forward. Now she rolled almost fully onto her starboard side. The starboard wing of the bridge, and then the funnel, went into the water. There were roarings and crashings, a cloud of steam and screaming air escaping, cries and groans from passengers, crew and rescuers – and then the bow, the whole ship, suddenly slipped beneath the water.

When Captain Vorobyov reached the ferry, and had seen the last of the passengers off his lifeboat being cared for by the *Arahura* crew, he was met by a young officer and invited to the bridge. Everyone was quiet.

Captain Brew, Captain Vorobyov and Captain Jamison, had each watched the ship's final moments in silence. No words were adequate to express the feelings of these three men.

"When a ship of that size and quality goes down, all one can feel is a great sadness. And when you are confronted by another captain who's just lost his ship, it's a terrible thing, terrible," Captain Brew recalled later.

Now, when they were all on the bridge, he asked the Russian, "Captain, is there anything you need?"

"Yes, I would like to use your VHF radio to check on my passengers and crew."

It was too crowded on the bridge. Captain Brew took the Russian master and his senior officers to his adjoining cabin, where he opened a bottle of whisky and ordered a tray of coffee for them. He invited the Russians to help themselves, and returned to the bridge.

Among the officers still on the bridge was Don Jamison. Although the two men had known each other for years it would have been inappropriate for John Brew to ask what had happened. He simply asked the pilot how he was, and if he needed anything.

Captain Jamison replied he was not injured, but said he couldn't get away from a Russian officer who had been following him closely ever since the ship struck. "I can't even go to the head without him following me," the pilot said.

Captain Brew found that degree of intrusion intolerable. "You can on my ship," he said. He directed the pilot to the toilet attached to his own cabin.

As the Russian made to follow, Captain Brew barred his

way. "Away, out you go," he said sternly. The Russian looked him in the eye for a few seconds. He may not have understood the words, but the authoritative gestures of a captain on his own bridge were enough. Whatever his own beliefs or orders were, he was professional seaman enough to recognise the ultimate authority of a master aboard his own ship. He turned away.

Immediately after the sinking, while the roaring of escaping air continued, they went into the business of finding out where all the ship's officers and crew were, and how many passengers had to be accounted for.

The bridge was crowded. Captain Jamison's son, who had happened to be a passenger on the *Arahura*, had joined him. The Russian chief purser, whose English was particularly good, was foremost with the lists of those who had to be counted.

Radio calls poured in, while the Russians in particular wanted to send calls out.

"It was such a busy and demanding time that it was no occasion for giving way to feelings or examining our emotions," John Brew was to say.

As those aboard the *Arahura* had watched the last minutes of the *Mikhail Lermontov*, there was near-silence. And as she finally slid down into the water and out of sight, nobody moved as they all tried to come to terms with what they had just witnessed. "My stomach just dropped," Faye Dickson said later. "There was a sense of disbelief."

The Heberleys, still searching for rafts and survivors, had been about 100 metres from the stern when the ship began to sink. Their jaws fell as they watched, transfixed. At this stage the rescuers believed about 70 people were still unaccounted for, and the Heberleys didn't know if some, all, or none of these people were still on board.

A huge steel container of frozen food which had been on the top deck fell down and crashed through railings before hitting the water.

Joe Heberley found the noise "just unbelievable". All the

air inside the ship had to get out somehow. Steam and air roared out, and bubbles, six to eight feet in diameter, burst up and out of the water, while deck chairs fell off decks and were tossed in the air again.

Joe Junior was transfixed by one particular sight: "The water fell out of the swimming pool!"

With a few lights somehow still on in the mid-section, but otherwise totally blacked out, the huge ship finally disappeared from view with a furious upheaval of foaming water, deck chairs, ropes and abandoned luggage.

Some objects were hurtled skywards as if launched by a catapult from beneath the surface as the ship went deeper down.

The ship went down bodily, listing heavily to starboard and by the head. Then the *Lermontov* lay right on her side, and disappeared.

Roaring and crashing came up from the depths for minutes afterwards as the ship settled in her grave.

A few minutes earlier, David Baker and Denis Cox had pulled their dinghy a good 50 metres away, to be clear of falling debris.

Containers of frozen food, which had been stored on deck, had tipped over the ship's side, spilling their contents into the sea. Other loose deck fittings had begun sliding off the pitched deck into the turbulent water. They listened, awstruck, to the scream of twisting steel and the crash of collapsing bulkheads. All this mixed and combined with the roar of air forced out of the ship by invading water. It made a terrifying noise, one which they would hear in their sleep for many months to come.

Escaping air kept the surface of the water boiling long after the ship had disappeared. Even from deep in the depths came the muffled sounds of escaping air and crashing steel.

Large buoyant objects went on leaping out of the water, some flying several metres into the air.

The problem now for searchers was that they didn't know where the ship was.

The whole bay was now a mass of debris – deck chairs, lifejackets and other wreckage, and all pervaded by a heavy oily smell. The oil stuck to everything afloat, including the hulls of the boats searching. It was still raining, and the chances of elderly passengers surviving long in these conditions were slim if there were any in the water.

David Baker and Denis Cox carried on searching for survivors, but it seemed a hopeless task, and they returned to the *Nimrod*. There Dave Fishburn had taken on some 30 survivors and was heading for the *Arahura*. They tied their own dinghy to the stern of the fishing boat so they could set about helping the passengers into the ferry's lifeboats, to haul them aboard.

This underlined for them how little chance any of these passengers would have had if they'd fallen overboard. They were all elderly, a few so frail they had to be lifted bodily off the fishing launch into the lifeboats. Some were nursing injuries. They were frightened, confused and close to exhaustion.

As the last of the elderly people were helped into the *Arahura's* lifeboat to be hauled up, one of them called out, "Three cheers for the *Nimrod*!" In the conditions it was the only way they could express their thanks to the crew of the little boat who had worked hard to get them to safety. It was a gesture from another age and another generation, but everyone on the *Nimrod* later agreed they felt goose bumps as the cheers rang out.

When the *Nimrod's* passengers were safely aboard the ferry, Dave Fishburn joined several other craft rounding up drifting lifeboats to tow them to one of the Navy ships.

The experienced small boat operators of the Marlborough Sounds became less than impressed with the Navy. While someone was passing a lifeboat towline to the patrol ship, the Navy captain decided to pull his ship ahead so the lifeboat could be added to the string of boats already tied to his stern. Instead of moving slowly the patrol ship surged ahead, and Dave Fishburn again had to take evasive action to miss a collision. Some earthy compliments on seamanship were exchanged but no damage had been done. They were later to learn that the *Taupo-class* patrol craft were not well designed for slow speed operations, and some of the harsh things they said that night about Navy skippers were probably somewhat unfair.

The *Nimrod* joined a shore search, using the launch's powerful light. The men believed they were looking for bodies, but they didn't know how many people might have died. Metre by slow metre they cruised along the rugged and inhospitable shore. Lifejackets, ropes and deck chairs were washing up, and each shape appeared, at first glance, to be a huddled body.

Body bags in fact arrived before 11pm, aboard the fishing boat *Swiftsure* which was owned by the Guard brothers of Port Underwood. John Guard was away, but Edward Guard and his crewman, John McManaway, had returned to Picton when the southerly blew up that afternoon. Blenheim police attached to Search and Rescue asked to be taken to Port Gore, together with medical supplies, food and body bags.

The *Swiftsure*, trying to dodge "the unbelievable junk" which seemed to cover the water, joined the flotilla of searchers, with some of the police transferring to other boats and trying to see, and impose, a pattern on the exhausting undertaking.

On board the ferry the wet and confused passengers were milling about in a mixture of relief, shock and confusion. Some of the more elderly simply fell asleep in the first warm, dry corner they found. Others, who had been injured, were being attended to by a nurse and a doctor who had been travelling on the ferry.

Many other ferry passengers were pitching in to help the *Arahura's* crew look after the survivors, distributing blankets and generally making the distressed survivors as comfortable as possible.

Lee Young was reunited with entertainer Bunny Gibson. They were sensible and experienced, and Lee had survived two strandings. They stuck close to a Russian bartender who'd had the presence of mind to salvage a bottle of vodka. By the time they got to Wellington, any stress Lee and Bunny had been feeling was considerably diminished.

Lorand Loblay was reunited with his companion, and was further warmed by the sight of scotch, brandy, beer and all manner of liqueurs, laid on for the passengers. Barman Ray O'Neill, in between dispensing hospitality, took some graphic photographs of the extraordinary scene.

The Russian crew continued to give comfort and assistance to passengers, while the *Arahura's* caterers were furiously busy providing hot food and drinks for both the survivors and the regular passengers, who would be hours late in getting to their destinations. Supplies of the ferry's main fare were soon close to running out, but soup by the gallon and hundreds of loaves of toasted bread were equally welcomed by the passengers. Most had had nothing to eat for some 12 hours.

The two Julies, on the *Tarihiko*, were just grateful to be safe. The tanker's crew quarters were brimming over with people, and again Julie Smith needed to be outside to ease her mind. She was hungry, but realised the tanker was not equipped to feed the extra hundreds it had taken on board. In fact food *was* being served, but to Julie it seemed the only thing on offer was warm beer. She wondered how long it would take them to get to Wellington.

Captain Brew had used his initiative and expertise to co-ordinate the rescue of passengers and crew from the liner. Now, knowing that wasn't the end of the matter, he returned to the main cabin to rejoin the Russian master.

Using the check lists Captain Vorobyov had brought with him, they faced the long and frustrating task of trying to account for both passengers and crew. On the *Arahura*, the forward lounge had been cleared for the survivors, but they were milling about so much it was impossible to count them with any accuracy.

At this stage it seemed that up to 60 people were missing. They could have gone down with the *Mikhail Lermontov*.

Vorobyov also didn't know the whereabouts of all his

officers. Some were aboard the *Tarihiko* but he didn't know how many. He ticked off each member as the name was verified by his officers on the *Tarihiko*, the *Arahura*, and the motor tender which was still searching in the darkness.

There still appeared to be about 60 people missing. Then over the VHF radio on the bridge came a message which brought enormous relief. One of the lifeboats with two others in tow was heading back towards Cape Jackson.

"Ask *Taupo* to go after them and see what they are up to. I think the last passengers are coming aboard now, and I don't want any more delays," Captain Brew said.

The naval patrol ship raced after the lead lifeboat, which was chugging off into the darkness, to find out where they thought they were going. At first the Navy's enquiries were simply ignored. Russian sailors don't like to be told what to do by members of other navies – Royal or otherwise.

After persistent questions there was much arm-waving, and the word "Picton", indicating they had been ordered to take whatever survivors they could find and head for the town of Picton, where they had been earlier that day. They had no idea how far away it was, or even if they had enough fuel to get there. Like good seamen they were obeying orders.

Captain Brew stepped through to his cabin and asked the Russian master if he could get his crewmen to return to the *Arahura* to be picked up.

A hint of a smile crossed the Russian's weary face. He was proud of the loyalty and bravery of his crew, and, using a hand-held VHF radio, he called them back. They were the last survivors to be brought to safety.

When the last passengers and crew members from the wayward lifeboats were safely aboard, the *Tarihiko* and the *Arahura* headed out of Port Gore for Wellington. In the rain and darkness they left behind lifeboats, liferafts and the still bubbling sea above the ship, a sea littered with personal luggage, deck chairs and anything else that could float. On the bottom the ship still heaved and rumbled as she settled into the sandy resting place she would share with the crewman,

Parvee Zagliadimov.

The small boats still searching could see the *Tarihiko* and the *Arahura* turn away from the scene and steam slowly out of the bay. Somehow the message that a lifeboat full of people had been found hadn't got through to them. Left behind, the searchers were surprised to experience feelings of isolation, shock and numbness. They kept listening for calls of distress, but heard only the sea and muted rumblings from the ship on the bottom. Here and there lights swept across the surface of the dark water, but they highlighted only empty lifejackets and wreckage.

By 2.30am no bodies or survivors had been found. Commander Robert McKillop of the Navy patrol ship *HMNZS Wakakura*, who had taken over control of the site after the *Arahura* departed, passed a message to all boats in the bay to settle down for the night. They would begin searching again at first light. He told the searchers that indications from Wellington suggested there could be up to 70 people missing.

In spite of the tragic scene that the searchers felt certain waited for them at daylight, the break was a welcome relief from their wet and chilling task. Joe Heberley, as a fisherman and head of the area's Search and Rescue team, was well used to bad conditions at sea, but what they'd just been through he called "hours of sheer hell". About six of the local fishing boats rafted up, and their crews with police and other volunteer searchers aboard shared drinks and accounts of the night's events. The *Nimrod*, as a fishing launch available for charter, was as usual well equipped for nights at sea.

Then, about 3am, came news that apparently everyone was accounted for. First relief, then exhaustion, overwhelmed them all. They would still search in the morning, but for now it was a matter of trying to make themselves comfortable for what was left of the darkness.

The three Heberley men on the *Fugitive* stumbled below. Then, "like Goldilocks and the three bears", they discovered – stretched out in their bunks – police from Blenheim, sound asleep.

CHAPTER EIGHT
Wellington

OUT in Cook Strait the cold rain continued, driven by the freshening southerly wind which now confined itself to lashing the windows and portholes along the *Tarihiko's* starboard side. She headed eastwards for Wellington, 50 miles away across Cook Strait. The *Arahura* was invisible, but not far astern.

Between them the two ships were carrying more than 700 exhausted passengers and crew from the Russian cruise ship. Nobody was quite sure how many. It was almost 3am, and the strain was having its inevitable effect. On the *Tarihiko*, Captain Reedman was worried about the several hundred passengers who were crowded into every available bunkroom and office, and even the passageways. What if they suffered from seasickness? But, in spite of the southerly, Cook Strait was comparatively, and mercifully, calm. After a quick check to see everyone was in as little discomfort as possible, he returned to his bridge.

The *Mikhail Lermontov's* second mate, Sergey Gusev, was looking out morosely into the rain and darkness. "Not a good day for you," Captain Reedman said, to break the silence.

"No, a very bad day," the Russian replied in clear English. "All I saved was my electric razor." He showed the captain this sole surviving possession. His face took on a puzzled expression. "How could a pilot run a ship onto the rocks, in his own waters, in clear weather? How could he do that?"

"I don't know," was all Captain Reedman could reply. "I don't know."

He was kept busy through the rest of the crossing trying to locate people, as requests for reassuring contact came by radio from distressed relatives.

In the galley his tired team had cleaned out virtually all their small store of food to provide drinks and snacks for the survivors. When everything which could be done had been, some of the crew were able to relax, or at least rest.

His passengers had frantic anxieties and griefs which no crew could have helped them with. The anguish for those with missing loved ones increased by the hour. Families had been split by the accidents of rescue. Precious possessions had also gone down with the ship. The sound of quiet weeping mingled with the murmur of talk as people tried to comfort one another.

Harry Thomas had held back at the cry of "Women and children first!" He had become separated from Jean, and their liferafts had gone in different directions. Harry had no way of finding out if Jean was on another ship or floating about in a lifeboat, or even if she was still alive.

On the *Arahura*, Jean Thomas was tormented by the same despairing thoughts as Harry was. She had last seen him waving to her from the ship. Had he got off safely before it went down? She didn't know and there was no one to help her. She felt alone, lost and completely powerless. Together they could face almost anything, but apart from him she was as frightened as a lost child. All she could do was pray.

Others aboard the *Arahura* were doing the same thing, some quietly, others aloud in groups. They too were going through the agony of fearing their missing partners or friends had been lost in the darkness and drowned. Some had been injured while transferring between lifeboats. They knew how easily they could have died; there was no reason to suppose all their stories would have happy endings.

Old, lightly covered shins had scraped against the sides of small boats. Stiff joints and muscles had been pulled and strained clambering to safety in the wet, cold darkness. Some cried out involuntarily, but few complained.

Ray and Lorna Leihn had taken John and Steven to the *Arahura's* cafeteria where toast and soup had taken the edge off their shock. The boys had been ravenous. They had missed dinner, and had a frightening adventure. The long night had finally caught up with them after they had eaten and they'd fallen asleep in their damp clothes, in the warm lounge.

Their bone-weary grandparents had settled down to get

what rest they could, huddled in fitful sleep under blankets and coats. It had been a terrifying experience but it was almost over. Ahead lay Wellington, dry clothes, proper sleep, and, they hoped, good news of the missing friends they had made on the voyage. Good news of everyone.

Hectic preparations for the ships' arrival had been underway in Wellington for hours. Nobody locally had organised such a huge operation before.

Police Inspector Wayne Strong had called an urgent meeting of senior people from the Soviet Embassy, the Australian High Commission, Australian Police Liaison, Wellington Free Ambulance, Civil Defence and George Scales Limited, (the New Zealand agents for the ship's charterers, CTC Cruises). Inspector Strong knew there would be confusion with such a big operation. He wanted to eliminate as much of it as possible, and establish a clear chain of command and co-ordination before the two ships arrived.

After getting agreement on which agency would be responsible for the various costs involved in the reception operation – not a small part of any problem once the initial rush to save lives was over – he managed to get the consent of all parties to let the police take full charge. It was a major achievement, because arguments over jurisdiction, particularly with significant costs involved, would have made the task close to impossible.

From the very beginning of the tragedy there had been frustration and confusion. It had been created by the unwillingness of the Russian officers to respond adequately to radio messages. It had been difficult, nearly impossible, to find out what was happening.

Authorities in Wellington had been unable to plan a large-scale rescue operation properly. The airwaves had quickly become jammed with confused and contradictory messages, so radio traffic became all but useless.

Apart from the language difficulties, the Russians seemed to have spent more time in contact with the USSR, on the other side of the world, than in trying to communicate effectively with rescue co-ordinators 50 miles away in Wellington.

The Russians had also ignored, or misunderstood, instructions on how to improve radio communications by using more appropriate channels. The Russian radio operators seemed to have a poor grasp of English. On the liner no-one seemed to have thought it was necessary to give them English-speaking assistants. Many incoming radio messages had not even been acknowledged.

Just before the ship had slipped below the surface, a final and futile SOS had been transmitted to Vladivostok. Perhaps it was politically necessary, but to New Zealanders trying to help it seemed ludicrous and almost deliberately insulting.

Poor radio communication and, in some cases, leaving passengers alone and literally in the dark, marred the Russian efforts in the rescue operation. But the crew's courage and devotion to duty were beyond dispute. Without the determination of Captains Brew and Reedman to get the passengers on to their ships, however, the bravery of the Russian crew in getting all the passengers safely off the sinking liner could have been for nothing. The loss of life would have been appalling.

One of the more frustrating results of poor communication had been confusion and disagreement about where the passengers would be taken. Before the *Arahura* and the *Tarihiko* reached Port Gore, Captain Vorobyov had intended to put people ashore there, and he had sought information about what buildings they could use as shelter while waiting to be taken by road to Blenheim.

The idea had been abandoned when he was told there was not enough shelter in the few farm buildings. The journey to Blenheim, too, would have taken about four hours across steep country, in four-wheel drive vehicles. Only a few of them were locally available, in any case. The idea of getting more than 700 people, more than half of them elderly, many with injuries, to Blenheim by road, had been simply unachievable.

With radio messages about beaching the cruise ship, the Rescue Co-ordination Centre in Wellington had then assumed the passengers would have to be picked up from the beach, and had decided the best option would be to take them back to Picton in the lifeboats and other small boats. This had been relayed to Inspector Roger Winter and his staff of 48 police officers in Blenheim and Picton, who in turn assumed they would be reinforced by police from Wellington.

A quick call to Woodbourne, the Air Force base and civil aviation airport near Blenheim, had soon had all personnel turned out and preparing. Feeding and caring for several hundred people was going to be a massive task. Every available person would be needed.

Assistance, including Russian interpreters, had been requested from Wellington, and the Air Force base was soon furiously busy. The possibility that the task might be too big for them never crossed their minds. Inspector Winter was not one to balk at difficulty, and he got all his officers on duty and busy.

The plan was for the small boats to be met in Picton and the passengers taken directly to Woodbourne, where temporary accommodation and medical services would be ready for them. In the rush, somehow Wairau Hospital, in Blenheim, was not officially alerted.

Doctor Jan Shapcott, the duty doctor in Picton that night, worried how the old Picton Hospital would cope.

When it was discovered that the passengers and crew were not on the beach, but safely aboard the *Arahura* and the *Tarihiko*, the logical decision by the Wellington rescue co-ordinators was to take everyone across Cook Strait to Wellington. But – somehow – Inspector Winter and his team were not told of the final decision until the ships had arrived in Wellington at dawn. Their mammoth effort had been for nothing except as a useful exercise in civil defence.

Picton police were not the only group who waited in vain for the lifeboats to arrive. A reporter and a photographer from

The Marlborough Express newspaper waited all night in a car for the survivors who never came. Deputy chief reporter Helen Hill had been at home playing Scrabble in Blenheim on that wet Sunday evening when she heard a report on the 6pm radio news about a ship in trouble in the Marlborough Sounds. She was duty reporter for the weekend. Her game was left unfinished. A big ship running aground was major news.

The Express, an afternoon paper, would have plenty of time on Monday for detailed reports and follow-up stories. Other newspapers, however, would be clamouring for details, and *The Express* had obligations to the New Zealand Press Association to file major news stories as soon as possible. She phoned deputy editor Frank Nelson at his home. "I'll see you in the office in about ten minutes," he said. After making what enquiries she could, Helen also called the chief reporter, Lynda Hooper, saying she would need a photographer.

Without radio contact with the ships in the Sounds, or with the Rescue Centre in Wellington, the news team could rely only on what their local police could tell them.

These amounted to four main points. The *Mikhail Lermontov* had struck rocks near Cape Jackson. The ship was to be run aground in Port Gore. All the passengers were to be taken off. Inspector Winter was preparing his staff at Woodbourne to take care of several hundred people, who were expected some time in the next few hours.

Helen Hill decided that sending a photographer out to Gore Bay by float plane could wait until Monday. The priority was to have someone at Picton when the lifeboats arrived. With that decision made, chief photographer Mike Boyle and Helen Hill set off from Blenheim in her car. Frank Nelson stayed in the office for a few hours, fielding calls from throughout New Zealand and Australia from newspapers and radio stations, all wanting details which the Blenheim news team did not have.

Helen and Mike went to the Marlborough Harbour Board offices, where they found assistant harbourmaster Gary Neill, and board chairman Bruno Dalliessi, who were also trying to find out what was happening.

Captain Neill had tried in vain to get clearance for the Cook Strait ferry *Arahura* to go to Port Gore when she left Picton around 8pm, and still didn't know if she had gone to help. He had heard no radio messages from Wellington Radio. Although willing to talk to the journalists, the assistant harbourmaster didn't have much to tell. Like everyone else, by then, he knew only that the ship was in trouble and seemed to be in need of assistance.

Bruno Dalliessi told Helen Hill that Don Jamison was aboard the ship as pilot. "But the Russian captain has complete control," he said. The four sat discussing the situation, wondering what to do. They could hear some radio conversations, and by 10pm it was obvious to Captain Neill that the *Mikhail Lermontov* was a doomed ship. He went down to Waitohi wharf and asked the crews of six volunteer boats, who had been waiting for a decision for several hours, to head for Port Gore and give what assistance they could.

Helen and Mike decided they would stay until the lifeboats arrived. They drove out to Karaka Point to wait. The point juts out from Whatamango Bay into Queen Charlotte Sound, eight kilometres to the east of Picton Harbour, and had once been a lookout point and pa for early Maori inhabitants of the area. From here, Helen thought, they would see the lifeboats coming up the Sound and have time to return to Picton to meet them.

They spent the rest of the night sitting uncomfortably in the car, waiting. Just as dawn was breaking, they gave up and returned to Picton. This was just before the era of cell phones, and they had been out of touch. Captain Neill and Bruno Dalliessi told them the passengers had been taken to Wellington instead. The ship had indeed gone down.

With little other prospect for news coverage, and as it was several hours before their office opened, they accepted an offer from Captain Neill to join him and Bruno Dalliessi on a flight out to Port Gore. They squeezed into the 30-year-old de Havilland Beaver float plane moored near the ferry terminal, and waited while the engine grumbled smokily into life and warmed up.

The taxi down Picton harbour was short and the powerful radial engine soon had them climbing out over the rugged Sounds terrain towards Port Gore. The wind had eased slightly but there were still air pockets to produce the occasional thump. On the way Helen talked with the assistant harbourmaster, who updated her, as far as he could, on what had happened while she had been waiting at Karaka Point.

Early on, Captain Reedman on the *Tarihiko* had been heard to make radio contact with the Russian master, but his offer of help had been declined. The *Tarihiko* had been on her way to New Plymouth but had diverted anyway. Captain Neill didn't know when the *Arahura* had got to Port Gore, as radio contact with the ferry had been lost when she reached Tory Channel.

Once they were over Port Gore they could see the huge, ghostly white shape, beneath the water, from which a stream of air bubbles and oil was flowing. A lifeboat was floating just below the surface, obviously still tied to the ship. The sea over a wide area was littered with ropes, lifejackets and the trash left behind when the big ship went down.

Here and there small boats were still fussing about among the wreckage, and – a striking sight of desolation – a Navy patrol craft had a string of empty lifeboats under tow. Mike took photographs, then it was time to get back and file their story. He and Helen, like so many others both on shore and off, had spent a long, tiring and confused night.

They felt sympathy for the rescuers in the small boats below them, weary from their exertions and not able to wing back to comfort.

There were some 25 small craft in the bay. Some were picking up oil-soaked items from the water, and parties from other boats were walking the beaches, searching among the rocks for bodies or survivors, but finding none.

Above them the searchers could hear the low familiar grumble of the Picton float plane, which had appeared out of the misty cloud to make several sweeps over the bay, but had not landed. Then came the thump of helicopter blades, arriving, they guessed, from Wellington.

Further out an RNZAF Orion aeroplane was making regular passes over the area. "There must still be people missing if the Air Force is out searching," someone called over the radio. The painstaking task continued.

About the same time, on the other side of Cook Strait, the two rescue ships nosed into a bleak Wellington Harbour.

The rain had eased to intermittent showers, but heavy grey cloud hung over the scene. The senior officers of both rescue ships, and many of their unhappy passengers, had been awake for more than 24 hours.

The central person in the setting up of the reception system was Police Sergeant Gordon Grantham. Under his direction he had 67 police officers, 13 civilians and 20 Russian Embassy staff. His untiring efforts and organisational skills were to win the praise and admiration of others involved in the Herculean task.

By this time the news had flashed around the world. Wellington was the centre of attention. Hundreds of telephone calls and fax messages poured into police national headquarters, adding to the already huge backlog of questions and queries from anxious relatives, mostly in Australia and New Zealand. Australian police set up their own phone number to filter calls, which reduced the volume coming into Wellington.

When Wellington city woke up to a wet Monday morning and the news of the drama which had been occurring in the Marlborough Sounds, another wave of phone calls flooded in. It even further overloaded the lines at police headquarters, and at the rescue centre.

This time the wave of calls was made up of offers of help from individuals and businesses. Far from being the impersonal political and commercial centre of the nation, Wellington showed it was a caring community at heart when hundreds of distressed people needed help. Homes and hot meals were offered by all and sundry. Several hotels were contacted; they made all their beds available. Some clothing stores volunteered to bring their entire stocks to the terminal immediately, and worry about payment later.

While organisers were moved by the outpouring of generosity, the scale of the operation made it impossible for the kindness of individuals to be accepted. It took several radio broadcasts to stop the calls of assistance coming in. Offers from clothing shops, however, were gladly taken up. Some people were lightly dressed in clothes still not really dry. Fresh, warm clothing was essential.

The *Tarihiko* was directed to the Overseas Passenger Terminal, where a complex system of reconciliation of people with passenger lists would have to be performed.

There had been a hold-up earlier in the arrangements while keys to the main building were located. The caretaker, who had the only complete set of keys to the building, had just moved house. No-one knew his new address or phone number. Personal pagers were, of course, reserved for 'important' staff. Someone at last tracked down his new address, and the keys were found. Then the planning operation was on course again.

In the early stages of planning the reception operation, the intention was for the *Arahura* to unload regular ferry passengers and the survivors from the *Mikhail Lermontov* at the ferry terminal. The planners realised, however, that having duplicate operations would stretch the already overloaded resources too far. Both ships must discharge survivors at the same berth.

The *Arahura* was hours behind schedule, and had a full load of freight and fare-paying passengers to discharge at the ferry terminal in spite of the extra distress the delay would cause those who had been separated. It seemed wise to have the regulars out of the way, reducing the congestion, before the several hundred distressed survivors from the liner were attended to.

As the regular ferry passengers walked down the gangway in Wellington, they looked shocked, as if they felt that what they had been a party to couldn't really have happened.

Faye Dickson remarked to her son, "I don't believe we saw all that!" She went to work but had to go home, suffering from what she thought was reaction. Hamish went off to school, thinking that nobody would believe him when he said he'd just seen a big cruise ship sink.

As soon as the fare-paying passengers and cars were safely ashore, ambulances drove onto the ferry to pick up injured survivors and take them to hospital. Captain Brew was very tired, but he still had several hours of work ahead before he could get any sleep. First the *Arahura*, carrying the rest of the survivors, had to go across the harbour to the Overseas Passenger Terminal. There the *Tarihiko* had almost completed disembarking the people she had rescued.

From the foot of the *Tarihiko's* gangway, three ambulances had taken away dangerously exhausted or distressed passengers. Of the hundreds of people involved, there was only one passenger with a broken bone, and only one with severe hypothermia. One man had a leg missing but this was not a new injury. He had lost his artificial leg when he'd been one of those who had to climb down rope ladders to reach a lifeboat.

On the wharf were the Salvation Army and Red Cross and Civil Defence people, and lines of police cadets who had been training for the visit of Queen Elizabeth the following week.

Inside the terminal five more ambulances were parked against the wall, with stretchers and chairs set out where survivors could be attended to. A number of elderly people had to be helped to these seats because they had stiffened up so much during their journey after their bumping and bruising escape from the sinking liner.

Too late staff realised it would have been useful to have had people available literally to lead some of the passengers from place to place, as they were checked off lists and allocated accommodation. Some people, who appeared perfectly well, nevertheless set off in the wrong direction or seemed not to understand simple instructions: such are the effects of prolonged stress and shock.

The Russian crew, predictably, suffered less. To begin with they were younger, and they had also trained for emergencies. Having to follow orders from foreign police, however, was not something they had been trained for. When police supervised them onto buses for transport to hotels, some arguments and mutually incomprehensible shouting matches took place as crew were split into smaller groups, but these reactions were soon sorted out.

A Red Cross caravan had been parked nearby to provide hot drinks. This became the main meeting place for separated family members and friends to come together again for the first time since they were taken off the *Mikhail Lermontov*, some 10 hours previously. Their relief and emotion at the reunion was overwhelming.

Harry and Jean Thomas both had tears streaming down their faces when they found each other. Their lost possessions and ruined holiday seemed trivial. They were together, and on dry land. Little else mattered. But the nightmares would return many times to haunt their sleep over the coming years.

At this stage it was still assumed there could be up to 70 people not accounted for, probably dead. Several times the passenger lists were checked against the names of those known to be safe, but there continued to be a serious discrepancy in the count.

With immediate comfort and medical needs attended to, a colour-coded series of information forms was completed. The first form everyone was required to fill in was blue for male passengers and non-Russian male crew, pink for female passengers and non-Russian female crew, and gold for all the Russians. When these had been dealt with, people went to the accommodation allocation desk where a further form, indicating where they were to go, was filled out in duplicate.

The top copy of the second form was pinned to the first form, and given to the team who were checking off the passenger and crew lists to see if, finally, all missing people could be identified. The duplicate was given to the person whose details it contained. There was also a scheme whereby people could send messages to family and friends.

And then, at last, buses took people off for some long-awaited simple luxuries such as baths, and rest.

The system mostly worked more quickly than its devisers may have imagined, because of the number of people working together to get this process out of the way. But, while the system later won accolades from authorities in various countries, a number of hold-ups and disputes occurred because of language difficulties and the effects of extreme tiredness. Many people had now been on their feet in extreme circumstances and without rest for more than 30 hours

The Leihn family were among the first to leave the Overseas Terminal. They were taken to a motel around 8am, so they could have some rest before a midday flight to Christchurch and a connecting flight to Australia.

They knew the news of the sinking would have reached home, and they wanted to assure their family they were all well. After a quickly 'tidy up' the foursome walked down the street to a telephone exchange. The boys were able to speak to their astonished mother about the events of the night.

Lorna Leihn was wearing a pair of borrowed slippers so they looked for a shoe shop. Ray wanted a dry packet of cigarettes. Luckily his wallet had stayed in his pocket and Australian currency was readily accepted.

As for the irrepressible Noeline Rodger, she soon found out what 'processing' meant.

"I discovered what it's like to be a refugee. You sit there with your hair all hanging down, and you wait and you wait."

Eventually she and Audrey Peterson were taken along the line of "these very nice young policemen" and were each handed a slip of paper which asked for their names and addresses and had these messages: 'Cruise ship has sunk.' 'I am fit and well.' 'Please contact...' with space for names of family or friends. Passengers were asked to fill out the forms and tick the messages.

But Audrey objected to their filling in the part about the cruise ship sinking. She didn't want to frighten anyone. "Don't say that. You can't say that. Cross that bit out. Just say 'fit and well'." They were told police would get messages to their families and friends.

Then began a little comedy of errors. These two women, having watched some Australians go off to the airport in "a very posh bus", were put with another group in a very old Road Services bus which broke down on its way out to the police college near Porirua. There they were eventually offered beds and food and more opportunities for messages to be passed on before being gathered together and told by the police commandant that they were all being taken to Christchurch, and then by jumbo jet to Sydney. Noeline politely explained that they didn't want to do that because they were New Zealanders. The commandant went away and conferred, and returned saying, "Well now. The Australians will go to the airport. The Russkies and the Kiwis will go to the overseas terminal." So back they went to where they'd arrived early that morning.

When they at last got out to the airport they had a different 90-year-old in their group. She was completely disoriented and was sure she was already in Auckland, so asked over and over why she was being told she was to fly to Auckland? Noeline thought she was "in danger of being strangled" so took her away and bought her a cup of tea. But she had no money to pay for it. That was soon fixed up. They were all also given money, enough for taxis at the other end.

By the time they disembarked at Auckland airport, Noeline, getting accustomed to VIP treatment, expected the Red Cross, the Salvation Army and probably mayor Dame Cath Tizard herself. There was nobody. Not a soul to meet them. None of the messages had got through.

The taxi delivered her home, with no more money after the fare, no luggage, not even a key to her own house. "But it was all right. I'd got another key planted in the garden."

Back at the rescue centre, results of the complicated head count began to narrow down the number of people thought to be lost at sea to about 20 passengers, and at least one member of the crew.

Calculations were confused, however, by 16 forms filled out for people who were not included on either list. The team went through the reconciliation process all over again, double checking their calculations. Enquiries were made at the hospitals where injured passengers had been sent.

Passengers were telling stories of at least one lifeboat leaving the scene with others in tow, and there was no way of knowing if this was the boat which eventually had turned back, or another boat altogether. There was also the possibility that different passengers had seen different boats disappearing in the rain. One lifeboat was known to be still tied to the ship. Could there be bodies in that? The Russian officers were unable to give an accurate count of the lifeboats.

Both Captain Vorobyov and Captain Jamison were nowhere to be found. A waiting Soviet Embassy staff car had swiftly driven Captain Vorobyov away, almost the moment he had stepped ashore, and Don Jamison had left the Arahura as soon as she had berthed. Unnoticed by the waiting throng of news media people, he had slipped away through the crowd, to disappear.

Various people also told of seeing at least one man fall into the sea, but none could remember seeing him picked up.

Then, around 1pm, waves of relief filled the Rescue Coordination Centre. The discovery was simple. The people who had joined the ship at Wellington and Picton had all filled in forms. These were extra people who were not on the passenger lists. Therefore, it was suddenly clear, the passengers named on the list, but for whom no forms had been filled in, had left the ship at its last two ports. The cause of all the confusion and alarm was, quite simply, that the passenger list had not been updated in the hours just before the calamity.

The missing persons list came down to two, a passenger and a crewman. The passenger, it was discovered, was John McLean of Sydney. He was the man who had fallen into the sea and been picked up by the Navy patrol boat *Taupo*. He had been the only passenger to be taken to Picton.

The crewman was refrigeration engineer Parvee

Zagliadimov, who, it would seem, had died immediately after the ship struck the rocks.

His body has never been recovered.

An Air Force Orion had set off before dawn to check for possible missing lifeboats. Its electronic searching ability was up to date and efficient. It established, rapidly, that there were no lifeboats in the search area. Rafts, of course, would not show up on radar. The search went on, and during the morning what Joe Heberley thought looked like a regular armada of boats arrived, to see whatever there was to see, and perhaps to help.

By mid-day the news came through to the small boats in Port Gore that there was nobody left to search for. It would have been a different story – "carnage", Joe said later – if the ship had sunk rapidly when it first hit the rock at Cape Jackson.

Some of the searchers began to recover things that might be salvagable – but they would later spend a lot of time cleaning the black oil off their boats. The Heberleys picked up a couple of the big lifeboat oars, and a few lifejackets. They found that some of the jackets could be torn with their hands, and were shocked. But, as James Heberley noted, at the end of the day the lifeboats, lifejackets, and the Russian crew had "done a good job of getting the people off the ship".

It had been a remarkable feat of combined small-boat skills by local fishermen, and professional seamanship by the masters and crews of the *Arahura* and the *Tarihiko*, and the *Mikhail Lermontov* herself, to get the remaining 737 people, more than half of them elderly, off to safety. Now it was all over.

The weary crews headed their little boats for home, leaving only the police launch *Lady Elizabeth II* to guard the site. Many men had missed a day's fishing and others had farm work to do.

At the Bakers' homestead, Tony and Betty were still at the radio sets, answering phone calls from all over the world. They had manned the radios without a break for nearly 20 hours, co-ordinating probably the most extensive, and far-reaching, rescue operation ever on the New Zealand coast. Both were dog-tired, but there was to be no rest until about 10pm, when they could stay awake no longer. Television interviews and more comments to the world's news media then had to wait.

The reconciliation operation in Wellington had taken until just past 1pm to complete; more than five hours of detailed, weary work. Some of the Australian passengers had been flown out of Wellington an hour earlier, to catch flights home from Christchurch.

The whole experience still seemed unreal. Thus Geoffrey Naughton, waiting in Wellington airport's departure lounge, had a strong urge to stand up on his seat and shout, "Hey everyone – I've been shipwrecked!" Unreal, yes. But he still had every intention of travelling by sea again.

Over the next few days all the passengers were flown home. All the passengers with one exception – Olive Edwards, of Sydney. She had come on the voyage with one over-riding intention, to see Milford Sound. It had been something she had dreamed of all her life, and she was not about to let the sinking of a Russian ship, or anything else for that matter, put paid to her dream.

She politely declined air tickets home, and she declined offers of alternative tours. She was going to Milford Sound, or every official from Wellington to Moscow and back again was going to hear about it. She steadfastly demanded that someone get her there, somehow. She didn't care how, but she was going, and there would be no argument about it.

Plainly something had to be done to satisfy this 74-year-old, and it was. New Zealand Railways, Dominion Breweries and the Tourist Hotel Corporation paid for her travel and accommodation, and she got to Milford Sound. There she took rolls of snap shots and thoroughly enjoyed herself. Nor had her appetite for cruise ship life diminished. She eventually sailed back to Australia aboard the *Alexander Pushkin*, one of the *Mikhail Lermontov's* sister ships.

Lee Young, flying back to Australia first-class (for the first time, he noted with pleasure), also took good post-disaster memories of Wellington with him. The Salvation Army had done a great job, and department store Woolworths had been generous.

He and Bunny Gibson had waited outside Woolworths until opening time to get new toiletries and underwear. They weren't sure how to deal with the fact that they had no money. They were grateful when Woolworths told them not to worry, just to accept the goods with the compliments of the management. Still doing their double-act of jokes and patter to keep spirits up, Lee suggested he and Bunny should visit an exclusive jewellery store on a similar mission. They tossed the idea around, but clean teeth won over old gold.

Some passengers were quite sure they would never again travel by sea. Shock and fear, however, could begin to give way to minor matters such as embarrassment. Wal and Jean Thorpe walked through two airports without realising that Jean's white slacks, which she had been wearing since the ship struck, had a very clear black imprint of a large hand on the seat, no doubt left by a Russian seaman as he helped her up the side of the *Arahura*. Hundreds of people must have seen the mark – but Jean didn't know about her branding until she got home.

Others suffered serious side-effects from their ordeal. These came to be called post-traumatic stress disorders. For many months people experienced symptoms ranging from frightening nightmares to mood swings and a confused state of mind. This left some sufferers unable to tell the difference between reality and their own fearful imaginings.

In the immediate weeks after the tragedy, every branch of the media seemed to have interviews and stories about the shipwreck. At home in Auckland, Noeline Rodger became increasingly angry about the "lack of openness" in what was told the public, and the unpleasant and "totally undeserved" criticisms which some people were making of the Russians.

She spoke out strongly, writing letters to editors – and complaining until the *New Zealand Herald* published one –

saying that shipwrecks were about people and not about politics. Because most New Zealanders and Australians were anti-communist, she said, that was blinding some of them to the great courage and unselfishness of the Russian crew. Everyone should know, and never forget, how magnificently they and the other rescuers had behaved. Other passengers rallied to support her. The rescuers' bravery was declared to be unsurpassed.

PART TWO

CHAPTER NINE

Captain Ponsford Investigates

CAPTAIN STEVE PONSFORD was on his way to his Wellington office on Monday morning when he heard that the *Mikhail Lermontov* had sunk in Port Gore in calm weather during the night.

As principal supervisor of ships for the Marine Division of the Ministry of Transport, Captain Ponsford was immediately involved in the drama of the night before, and the events which were still unfolding on the Wellington waterfront.

There had been no storm or high winds to endanger such a big ship. He was astonished to hear it had grounded at Cape Jackson before going down in Port Gore. Master mariners operating in the Marlborough Sounds were well aware of the areas of clear water and foul ground in the Sounds and gave risky regions a wide berth. The Sounds were well charted.

Captain Ponsford was even more surprised to learn that Picton harbour pilot Don Jamison had been on board the ship when she went aground. He had known Don Jamison for half a lifetime; the two master mariners were personal friends.

The director of transport, Jack Critchley, and the chief surveyor of ships, Eric Galloway, were waiting for him when he arrived at his office. The three held an urgent meeting to decide how the sinking would be investigated. Early reports indicated at least one fatality, with the possibility of more being confirmed when final figures were available.

Captain Ponsford was chief marine inspector, and it was to be his task to hold the preliminary enquiry, this in spite of his personal relationship with Don Jamison. Apparently nobody questioned a possible conflict of interest. While there was no direct political pressure, Transport Minister Richard Prebble also made it known he wanted the enquiry done quickly.

At the time of the sinking of the *Mikhail Lermontov*, New Zealand was in the international political wilderness. Under Prime Minister David Lange's Labour Government, all nuclear-powered and nuclear-armed warships had been barred from New Zealand waters. This had shaken the ANZUS Treaty to its core. The defence alliance was made up of Australia, New Zealand and the United States, but New Zealand was held to have effectively resigned from the relationship by stopping American warship from visiting.

Britain, also a major nuclear power, was still struggling to be accepted as part of the new-age Europe, so did not have a lot of time for its rebellious former South Pacific colony. Of the nuclear powers, only the Soviet Union, which also had a vast nuclear-powered and armed navy, wanted to trade freely with New Zealand but did not plan naval visits.

The Soviet Union, however, was short of international credit and was in debt to New Zealand for imports of primary produce. Offers to pay for this by trading industrial machinery and vehicles for at least some of it had been scorned by some, but taken seriously by others who maintained that payment in kind was not to be dismissed lightly when there were no other equivalent customers.

Fundamental to the situation, too, was the fact that the Soviet Union, with its communist bloc, was also still a major world power, whom nobody wanted to cross swords with, particularly when the New Zealand economy was undergoing a traumatic restructuring. There was also a deep-rooted suspicion of the Soviets and their communist masters, especially among the older generation who had watched anxiously as major world powers played dangerous games of brinkmanship during the Cold War years.

For Captain Ponsford the complexities of international politics provided a difficult backdrop for an enquiry into the loss of a liner, not to mention one which had apparently been piloted by his close personal friend, but it seems that no thought of disqualifying himself from the task crossed his mind. Both men were professional master mariners, and Ponsford had no doubts about his ability to find the cause of the tragedy, in spite of the fact that the public rumour machine was already almost in top gear.

Suspicions and dark conjectures began erupting from the moment the news broke:

> *A Soviet ship sinking in calm weather could not possibly have an innocent explanation...*
>
> *The officers on the bridge had been drinking vodka all day and were hopelessly drunk...*
>
> *They had put secret agents ashore in the remote wilderness of the Marlborough Sounds to infiltrate the community with sinister intent...*
>
> *The Russians had planted sophisticated listening devices in the ship before she went down, to keep track of New Zealand's defence plans now ANZUS was effectively ended...*
>
> *They had left homing devices on the* Mikhail Lermontov *to guide nuclear missiles launched from Russia...*

These were among the early rumours. They were to persist for years, and are still resurrected when talk turns to the *Mikhail Lermontov*: People say, "*We were never told the whole story.*"

After all, French agents had sunk the *Rainbow Warrior* at night while she was moored at an Auckland wharf. This incredible event, the deed of a 'friendly' foreign power, had taken place just over seven months previously. Here was something else to help reinforce the beliefs of those who love conspiracy theories.

> *New Zealand had pulled out of ANZUS, and was being punished by all and sundry. It was obvious...*
>
> *French agents had also sunk the* Mikhail Lermontov...

Captain Ponsford put no credence in rumours. He wanted facts, and to get on with his enquiry. Offices and clerical staff were hastily provided, and an interpreter, Boris Ashikhmin, was engaged to assist.

By 2pm on Tuesday 18 February, Captain Ponsford was ready to begin hearing the testimony of the Soviet master, his senior officers, and Captain Jamison, all of whom had barely begun to recover from the event itself. At least it was still fresh in their minds. He was determined to complete the task in a week.

Sitting with Eric Galloway alongside him, Captain Ponsford heard the first testimony. It was from the 47-year-old Russian master, Captain Vladislav Vorobyov, who had been staying at the Soviet Embassy since he stepped ashore from the *Arahura* in Wellington.

The Russian master, without embellishment or drama, outlined in detail the course of events which led to the loss of his ship. He detailed the two near-groundings in Shakespeare Bay and Golden Point, and his instruction to Captain Jamison to keep the ship further offshore.

In spite of these two instances Captain Vorobyov said he had agreed to let the pilot take the ship into Ship Cove without giving specific instructions about minimum distances off shore, and without a precise course marked on the chart of the Sounds. He explained about being wet and cold and going to his cabin to change before the ship reached Ship Cove. As he was cold he also took a shower, and was about to return to the bridge when the ship struck.

Captain Ponsford paused for a moment and then asked, "Can you please be candid and frank in your answer to this question?

"During your stay in Picton and during the period on the voyage from Picton to Cape Jackson in which you retired to your cabin, how much alcohol, if any, did you consume?"

The Russian looked directly at Captain Ponsford. "Since the ship left the Soviet Union, I consumed no alcohol whatsoever on board the ship," he said firmly. He concluded the first day of the hearing by saying the course the ship took prior to the grounding, as marked on the chart by his navigator, was to port of the course he had agreed to.

By now he had been giving evidence for nearly five hours

and was due to resume again in the morning.

The next day Captain Vorobyov described the final hours leading to the sinking of his ship, following the loss of both engines.

"After the engines stopped, the ship continued drifting towards the shore, and when it was eight cables from the shore, all way stopped.

"I asked the pilot regarding the tidal situation and he informed me that the tide should start rising in about half an hour as it was almost on low tide. I asked the pilot what measures were being taken ashore to assist the ship. He informed me that two ships had left Picton. He did not know what type of ships they were, but they were expected to arrive in approximately two hours. At that time, with my experience and the fact the list and trim were remaining relatively constant, I estimated the ship would remain afloat for that two hours and I expected that, on the rising tide, the ship would be carried towards the shore.

"At this time, an unexpected situation developed when I was informed by the chief navigator that the damage control parties had reported that, due to the list of the ship, some of the water-tight doors were not now fully closed, and the list had increased to 18 degrees. I realised the situation was critical.

"Through the chief navigator, I asked how many passengers remained on board. At that stage the ship's broadcasting system was still functioning. I was told that approximately 80 passengers were still on board. I also asked where they were mostly situated. I was informed that they were gathered mainly at the main embarkation door and the stern embarkation door on the port side.

"I gave instructions for all personnel in the engine room to leave the engine room as I expected the engine room would soon be flooded. Exactly ten minutes after instructing the engine room to be evacuated, the chief engineer came to the bridge and informed me that all crew had left it.

"After consulting with the chief engineer, the chief navigator and all the officers present on the bridge, I gave instructions for the crew to leave the ship. At this time the list was 20 degrees. I sent a seaman to the forecastle head to measure the depth of water at the bow by means of a sounding line, and then to measure the depth of water at the stern by the same method. He informed me that the depth at the bow was 21 metres and the depth at the stern was 43 metres.

"Myself and all the other officers on the bridge and the pilot watched intently the shoreline at Gannet Point, and we established the ship was drifting towards that point. When the engines stopped, the radar ceased to function. The echo sounder had ceased to function on the first shock off Cape Jackson."

Captain Ponsford interrupted the Russian master with a question. "As the ship was drifting in towards Gannet Point, did you use your anchors to stop the drift?" It was a question that would be asked hundreds of times in the years following the tragedy.

Captain Vorobyov answered clearly. "I did not use the anchors because I was hopeful the ship would drift into shallow waters off Gannet Point. The pilot supported my hopes, saying it looked possible that the ship would drift into shallow waters," he said.

Captain Ponsford also asked, "Why were the crew abandoning ship when there were still passengers on board?"

Again the Russian master was clear in his recollection of events. "At the time I instructed the crew to begin evacuation, there was a tender alongside the main embarkation door on the port side and a tender alongside the main embarkation door at the aft end. The remaining eighty passengers were mustered at these two doors, and there was sufficient space in two tenders to take all the remaining passengers," he said.

"All the other motor boats were en route to the gas carrier, and thinking of the safety of my crew, they started evacuation down the embarkation ladders into oar-propelled lifeboats.

"The crew, females first, started evacuating into these boats by the embarkation ladders. The remaining crew helped the passengers evacuate into the tenders. As the oar-propelled lifeboats became filled with crew members, they were rowed towards the gas carrier. Then I gave instructions for all persons on the bridge to evacuate, with the exception of the chief navigator, the purser, the second officer on duty, and myself. The other persons who were on the bridge, including the pilot, then proceeded to evacuate by lifeboat."

Captain Vorobyov explained how his crew had left the ship with only the clothes they were wearing and their passports after they had assisted all the passengers off. "I would like to add the evacuation of the crew was carried out very quickly, efficiently and without any panic," he said. He ended his second day of evidence by saying that all available blankets on the ship had been thrown into the lifeboats to help protect the passengers from the cold.

On Friday Captain Vorobyov asked to be able to add to his testimony and correct his estimate of the ship's final course into Port Gore, which was directly between two buildings at the southern end of the bay, and not in Tunnel Bay as he had earlier suggested. Captain Ponsford took the opportunity to question him closely on the last known sighting of the missing refrigeration engineer, who had by now been given up as lost with the ship.

"Captain, I would also like to clarify one point. When you gave the order to close the water-tight doors after the shocks, what was the time lapse between the time of the shocks and the time of closing the water-tight doors?"

"Possibly five but a maximum of ten minutes. Between five and ten minutes."

"Before giving the order to close the water-tight doors, what action was taken to ensure that all persons were evacuated from the forward damaged compartments in the ship?"

"The emergency party at the forward end of the ship was checking those compartments to evacuate any persons."

"The missing refrigeration engineer, to your knowledge when and where was he last seen?"

"He was last seen in the forward part of the ship near the refrigeration machinery. He was seen by four people working in the refrigeration stores which are adjacent to the refrigerated machinery compartment. He was last seen by those people five or ten minutes before the shocks."

"Can you tell me the name or names of the persons who last saw the refrigeration engineer?"

The Russian master was able to name only two people who had last seen the missing crewman, but said he was sure the Wellington police had the names of all four.

It had been a long and sometimes distressful recollection and questioning, and he was relieved that part of it was over. Now all he wanted to do was get home although he was sure a much more searching and severe enquiry would be held there – but at least he would be home.

The next officer to appear before the enquiry was Staff Captain Georgey Melnik, who had been the first to confirm Captain Vorobyov's fears that the ship could not stay afloat with the amount of water entering the rip in the hull. He had been in charge of damage control and the four emergency parties which had been activated immediately after the ship struck.

The 40-year-old senior officer was off duty and resting in his cabin directly below the bridge on the port side when he felt the impact. He rushed to the bridge to find other senior officers there ahead of him and the captain in command.

"The first report I received was that water was entering the garage, the refrigerated stores, the refrigerated machinery compartment, the laundry and the printing compartment. Number one hold was dry and the bow thruster compartment below number one hold was also dry.

"There were no reports of water entering the main engine room and also no reports of water entering the auxiliary engine. After that I gave an order for all persons to evacuate J and H decks from forward, aft as far as the refrigerated stores," he said.

Captain Melnik then went on to explain how he had concluded the ship could not remain afloat with the amount of water entering the damaged hull. He had ordered the number five port ballast tank, which was holding about 70 tonnes of water, and the swimming pool, which was holding an additional 50 tonnes, to be pumped out.

"I then received a report that water was entering the

stabiliser compartment and I understood from that that the damage was extensive," he said.

"All the pumps were working but they were not coping. The peculiarity of our ship is that when any two compartments are flooded, the ship will remain afloat. If the two biggest compartments are flooded, that relates to approximately 4,000 tonnes. In our present situation, I calculated that the amount was 7,000 tonnes."

To clarify the point Captain Ponsford asked, "With the ship in that position, making 7000 tonnes into watertight compartments, what was your estimate of the chances of remaining afloat?"

"The position at that time was that if those compartments were completely flooded, they would have contained approximately 7,000 tonnes but at that time they were not completely flooded and contained less than 4,000 tonnes and we would still have some time before they became completely flooded. The degree of list at that time was such that the portholes on J deck were above water and, therefore, water could not enter until they were submerged. I reported the situation to the captain and we realised the situation was very critical, and that it would be necessary in the shortest possible time to find a place to beach the ship."

Other officers gave their accounts of the events leading to the loss of the ship.

Then came Captain Don Jamison. He read a prepared statement on Monday 24 February, eight days after the tragedy.

His statement covered the events from his joining the ship in Wellington on the Saturday night, to his departure from the *Arahura* in Wellington on the Monday morning.

After detailing his experience and qualifications, Captain Jamison's statement read:

"I joined the *Mikhail Lermontov* in Wellington on Saturday 15 February at 1500 hours. The ship left Wellington at 2400 hours and I requested a call at 0500 hours and asked that the ship be at a certain position at 0600 hours. I went on the bridge around 0530 hours. The ship entered Tory channel about 0645 hours and I acted as pilot until the ship berthed at Picton.

"I have acted as pilot of other ships of similar size and larger including a sister ship to the *Mikhail Lermontov*. I was quite happy with the handling of the ship.

"I boarded the ship at 1450 hours on Sunday 16 February and she left Picton at 1500 hours. The deputy harbourmaster, Captain Neill, was on board for pilotage training purposes. The vessel was scheduled to cruise in Queen Charlotte Sound. On leaving Picton harbour the vessel turned towards Shakespeare Bay to view the remains of the *Edwin Fox*. Turning out of Shakespeare Bay I became concerned that the ship was not turning as fast as necessary.

"To assist the turn the starboard engine was stopped and put full astern. Full starboard bow thruster was ordered. The ship did not respond as anticipated and the port engine was put full astern. We pulled up approximately 30 metres from the shore and at right angles to it. I later learned that the bow thruster had not operated. Captain Neill told me it was not operational at the time it was first requested as the motor had been turned off. The bow thruster after being turned on was used to turn the bow to starboard and we proceeded up Queen Charlotte Sound for sightseeing purposes. I conned the ship rather than used a charted course. This was my usual practice.

"Whilst manoeuvring in Shakespeare Bay my feet slipped on wet gratings and I fell heavily on my back. My keys came out of my pocket and also my spectacles. The deputy witnessed this. The weather was southerly about 15 knots with three to four kilometres visibility.

"Towards the outer Sound we took a sweep into Ship Cove. During sightseeing I had given a commentary on the public address system. This was not heard on the bridge. Apart from the public areas I do not know where else it was heard. Sometime after leaving Ship Cove I made an announcement on the public address system. To the best of my recollection I said that was the end of my commentary for the day as we were leaving the Marlborough Sounds and I would be leaving the bridge and would resume my commentary when we reached Milford Sound the day after next. I referred to Cape Jackson coming up ahead.

"No arrangements had been made to relieve me and I continued to con the ship. The master was not on the bridge. The officer on watch took no part in navigation after leaving the pilotage area. The point of embarkation and disembarkation for a pilot is clearly marked on chart NZ615. I would expect the master of a ship to be familiar with this and also to have referred to the *New Zealand Port Manual* which gives details of pilotage areas. If after passing the outer limits of the pilotage area the master had appeared I would have taken steps to hand the ship back to him. I believe it is my responsibility to hand the ship back to the master. Had the master not appeared within a reasonable time I would have handed the ship back through the officer of the watch who I would expect to inform the master.

"I would not have handed it back to other than the master until the ship was in clear water. Until the master appeared on the bridge I intended to con the ship into the clear area around Walker Rock and then hand over to the officer of the watch. At this time it was light southerly and the rain had cleared.

"When the passage between Cape Jackson and the light opened up and when the vessel was approximately three-quarters of a mile south-east of Cape Jackson I made a sudden decision to go through the passage. I ordered port ten and started to go through the passage. This order was not questioned by the officer of the watch.

"The passage between Cape Jackson and the light is approximately three cables wide. I have been through the passage on many occasions on small craft and have often fished in the passage. I am aware that the passage is used by coastal vessels and I was of the understanding the depth of 35 or 40 feet existed in the passage close to Cape Jackson. I took a course close to Cape Jackson.

"After the ship had passed the headland and when I was considering a course for d'Urville Island, the vessel struck. At that time I believe we had passed through the passage and cleared Cape Jackson.

"The speed of the vessel at the time of the impact was approximately 15 knots. The ship took the course I intended and did not appear to be affected by any tidal stream.

"Within a very short time after the impact the master came on the bridge with other crew members and for a time there was confusion. From then on the master took complete charge.

"I am unable to understand why I made the sudden decision to pass through the passage.

"It was certainly not a planned course but a decision made on the spur of the moment and quite out of keeping with my normal behaviour. I have always considered myself to be a capable and competent pilot and believe that my abilities have always been held in high regard by those associated with the harbour industry.

"In hindsight the only explanation I can offer for the action I took is that I was suffering from mental and physical exhaustion and that I was over-stressed as a result of working long hours for an excessive period of time, and that as a result of such I was not in adequate physical or mental condition to be acting as pilot. Obviously I did not recognise that as I was in such a condition.

"On 1 October 1985, in addition to my position as harbourmaster I was appointed as acting general manager which position was vacant as a result of the harbour board previously dismissing the general manager. The deputy harbourmaster had left on 25 September to take up an overseas posting and his replacement, Captain G F Neill, did not take up his duties until 20 December 1985. Therefore from 1 October I was carrying the duties of general manager, harbourmaster, deputy master and pilot. In accepting the appointment I recognised it would involve considerable extra work and this could only be achieved by working extra hours. At the end of 1985 I kept a diary recording the hours worked. These hours averaged 75 to 80 per week. Basically I have worked between the hours of 0600 to 2200 or 2400 seven days a week. This level of work has continued up until the present time and of course I carried out these duties in addition to my duties as pilot.

"Additional to the hours actually worked and the duties performed I was always on call and only left my home port of

Picton to carry out official duties. It was necessary for me to cancel my plans for annual leave.

"At present I have sixteen weeks of leave due to me. On several occasions my wife has had to come to the office at midnight and insist that I return home.

"Whilst the appointment of a new deputy harbourmaster has relieved some of the work pressure it has created the additional stress of training a new staff member and I have been most conscious of the fact that I have not been able to devote as much time as I would like to this function.

"There have been additional stresses to cope with in that the general manager's dismissal has involved the board in a continual process of litigation which is still ongoing. This has had an unsettling effect throughout the board's staff and has made my job as acting general manager more difficult to perform.

"On Friday 14 February I worked in my office until 2300 hours. I was back at the office at 0700 hours on Saturday and worked through until 1345 hours when the deputy harbourmaster picked me up to go to the airport. We travelled to Wellington and joined the vessel for pilotage to Picton. I was called at 0500 hours on Sunday.

"After the arrival of the vessel at 0800 hours I worked all morning in the office, particularly endeavouring to arrange for a pilot to be available if required during the week I was away. At 1200 hours the chairman and myself attended on board the vessel to make a presentation to the captain. I then had a hurried lunch, leaving the vessel at 1345 hours to complete work at the office and returned on board at 1450 hours for a 1500 hours departure.

"By the time we reached the outer pilotage limits I must have been extremely tired although I did not realise it. This probably affected my judgment. I referred to the fall I had on the deck while the vessel was in Shakespeare Bay. I did not remember the fall until reminded of it by my deputy some days later. I suffered a sore neck and back the day after the stranding and now realise it resulted from the fall. This arose out of my discussion with the deputy harbourmaster about the failure of the vessel to turn in Shakespeare Bay. It was of considerable surprise to me to be told that the bow thruster initially failed to operate at Shakespeare Bay because it had apparently been turned off and I did not appreciate that it had not worked when I ordered it.

"After the impact and after the master had taken charge I remained on the bridge. I manned the VHF radio. The master asked where the vessel could be beached and I advised Ship Cove or Port Gore. The master chose Port Gore. I started to keep notes of events and radio communications. These notes were left in the wheelhouse. I advised Wellington Radio that the ship had struck a rock and had starboard list and that we had a Mayday situation and that the position was being assessed. Wellington Radio ZLW asked me to confirm that it was a Mayday call. I referred this to the master who said it was not a Mayday situation and that assistance was not required. I did not agree with this assessment but did not argue with him and advised ZLW accordingly. He also said he did not want assistance. I asked ZLW to record the time of this message.

"I contacted Picton Harbour Radio to check with a member of the launch crew the state of the beach at the head of Port Gore and the best landing place. I knew he was familiar with the area. He confirmed my understanding of the nature of the beach. The vessel made its way into Port Gore under its own power at approximately five knots. There was a gradual increase in the starboard list. I felt the situation was worse than was being made known by the master.

"At some stage I provided the master, at his request, with a copy of chart NZ 615 which I obtained from my cabin. He apparently only had a small-scale Russian chart of the area. The master was proposing to anchor at the south-east head of Port Gore at about Gannet Point, and the engines failed and the ship carried away until it grounded in the south-east corner of the bay west of the homestead. It was a very light grounding and the ship stopped about a ship's length off the shore.

"The LPG tanker *Tarihiko* arrived on the scene before the grounding. She offered to take passengers off on her boats.

This offer of assistance was declined. I eventually on my own initiative suggested that the master of the *Tarihiko* put his boats in the water and come over. He did this. Most of the time I was in the wheelhouse and could not see outside activity. After the vessel grounded it crossed my mind that anchors should be dropped. The vessel drifted along the beach in an easterly direction but still in shallow water. With a change in the wind she later drifted off the beach and back into deep water. At the master's request I ordered a tug.

"The master wanted to be pushed up further onto the beach. I advised that two tugs were coming and he advised that he only wanted one tug. I advised Wellington accordingly. The master requested the *Tarihiko* to push the ship onto the beach but the *Tarihiko* declined as she was not gas-free and her draft was considered too great.

"I did not observe all activity on the ship as I spent most of the time in the wheelhouse with the radio and it was completely dark outside. I observed some lifeboats along the port side and in the water and they were there for a considerable time. Whether they were port or starboard boats I do not know. I also saw a motorised boat ashore, apparently checking the landing location. There was difficulty in launching the inflatable liferafts on the port side due to the heel. I did not see any of the liferafts operate once they had been launched. There were about six canisters in the water unopened.

"I was not in a position to observe the disembarkation until I was directed below under observation by a crew member. There was congestion at the first door I was sent to and we were sent to another door. The angle of heel was about 20 degrees. People were having difficulty in climbing stairs and keeping on their feet. They did not appear to realise the gravity of the situation.

"I disembarked into a ship's lifeboat and was towed to the *Arahura*. The ship was illuminated by the *Arahura's* search light and I could see no-one aboard when I left. By the time we reached the *Arahura* the ship had sunk. The *Arahura* left the scene at about 0300 hours and proceeded to Wellington. I travelled on the bridge of the *Arahura* and saw nothing further of the passengers..."

As Captain Ponsford had known Don Jamison for many years and was aware of his ability as a pilot, he questioned him at length about key events in the saga. He wanted to know in particular what the pilot's employment arrangements were on the day the ship was lost.

Captain Jamison said, "My duty for the Marlborough Harbour Board was to act as the pilot within the pilotage district of the board. This district extends in a line 303 degrees from Paparoa Point, across the northern end of Motuara Island to the opposite shore. After passing outside the pilotage area I had no further responsibility to the Marlborough Harbour Board, and on the voyage in question I commenced a period of leave from the point where my responsibilities ceased.

"In accordance with normal board practice I had lodged an application for leave with the board secretary from this point. I intended to travel with the ship to the Fiordland area where I was to act as coastal pilot under my coastal pilot's licence."

"Apart from your pilotage responsibilities in the areas you have mentioned, did you have any type of agreement or contract with the master of the *Mikhail Lermontov* to act as pilot or advisor beyond those limits?"

To this Don Jamison answered, "No." He went on, "I was then to travel on to Sydney and then return to my duties with the Marlborough Harbour Board on the expiry of my leave."

"Please give the requested position of the ship at 0600 hours on Sunday 16 February and what time you assumed your pilotage responsibilities?"

"The position requested was approximately three miles south-east of Tory Channel entrance representing an appropriate position for me to be on the bridge prior to the approach to Tory Channel entrance. As it was necessary to delay the entrance to Tory Channel I recommended the vessel should steam south for approximately 20 minutes. The vessel was then turned around and steamed back towards Tory Channel entrance. There was no formal handing over but I took over the con of the vessel as it approached Tory Channel entrance."

"Which of the *Mikhail Lermontov's* officers were on duty on the bridge at the time?"

"I do not know which officers were on the bridge. One officer did express concern at the late entry and our approach to Tory Channel as they considered this would result in the vessel being late alongside at Picton. The delay in entering Tory Channel was necessitated by previous advice from the vessel's agent that he had engaged a helicopter and proposed to take photographs of the vessel as it entered Tory Channel. Furthermore the final time of entry was timed so as to pass the outward-bound *Aratika* between the Tory Channel entrance and Clay Point. There had been discussions by VHF with the *Aratika* after the ship entered Tory Channel at 0645 hours. I continued to act as pilot until the ship berthed at Picton. I have acted as pilot for other ships of similar size and larger, including a sister ship of the *Mikhail Lermontov*. I was quite happy with the handling of the ship."

"After your fall in Shakespeare Bay were you physically or mentally impaired due to the fall?"

"I do not recall being so. However I did not remember the fall until reminded of it several days later by the deputy harbourmaster."

"What were the charts in use at the time and did you refer to them during the passage up the Sounds?"

"I did not use any charts of my own. I did not know what charts the vessel was using as I do not recall going into the chartroom where presumably any charts they were using were kept.

"The weather at Shakespeare Bay was southerly about 15 knots. My deputy left the ship in the vicinity of Curious Cove."

"What time was that?"

"I would estimate 1630 hours. Sometime after the deputy left the ship the master left the bridge. After turning the vessel in Shakespeare Bay I suggested to the master that in view of the poor weather the passengers would not be very interested in sightseeing and that I considered the best programme would be for us to slowly make our way out of Queen Charlotte Sound.

"In suggesting this I had intended that the vessel cruise in the Grove Arm which is west of Shakespeare Bay. This has normally been done when vessels have been cruising but due to the weather conditions I considered it would be a waste of time from a passenger enjoyment point of view. That was the only discussion I had with the master as to the departure programme for the vessel."

"What was the intended track of the vessel after leaving Queen Charlotte Sound?"

"I had not planned any course or intended track for the ship after it left the pilotage district at Motuara Island. After the master had left the bridge, the location of which I am unsure, there remained on the bridge at least one ship's officer and the helmsman. At all times the helmsman was competent. I was not aware of any other person acting as lookout. Towards the outer Sound we took a sweep into Ship Cove. While sightseeing I had given a commentary on the public address system. This was not heard on the bridge apart from the public areas and I do not know where else it was heard. In saying that, I could occasionally hear my comments floating out from the boat deck. Some time after leaving Ship Cove I made an announcement on the public address system. To the best of my recollection I said this was the end of my commentary for the day as we were leaving the Marlborough Sounds and I would be leaving the bridge and would resume my commentary when we reached Milford Sound the day after next."

"At that time did you enquire of the officers on the bridge as to arrangements for your relief by the master or one of his officers?"

Captain Jamison said he had not made any such enquiries. He also said the officer on watch had taken no part in the navigation of the ship after it left the pilotage area.

"The point of embarkation and disembarkation for a pilot is clearly marked on chart NZ615," Captain Jamison said.

"To your knowledge were charts NZ615 and NZ6153 and

the *New Zealand Port Information Manual* on the *Mikhail Lermontov* at the time?"

Captain Jamison said he did not know what charts were on the ship. "I subsequently became aware that the vessel did not have a copy of chart NZ615, as after the stranding the master asked me to get my own copy which was down below in my cabin. The reason for the master asking for this chart was that he had in front of him a small-scale chart of the Cook Strait area, of Russian origin."

Question after detailed question was put to the pilot who rarely departed from the contents of his prepared statement. Captain Ponsford pressed the pilot particularly on the reason why he had not handed over the command of the ship to the master or a senior officer at the end of pilotage limits when the ship was still in open water.

"If after passing the outer limits of the pilotage area the master had appeared I would have taken steps to hand the ship back to him. I believe it is my responsibility to hand the ship back to the master. Had the master not appeared within a reasonable time I would have handed the ship back to him through the officer of the watch who I would expect would inform the master."

"At the time you made the sudden decision to manoeuvre the ship through Cape Jackson Passage, did you inform anyone on the bridge of your decision?"

"No, I gave the whole instruction to the helmsman."

"Prior to that time had you previously conned any ship through the passage? And, if so, please give details of the previous ships and times."

"I have never conned any large vessel through the passage. I have been through the passage on many occasions in small craft with drafts up to two metres and I have often fished in the passage."

"Do you have a personal knowledge of the soundings and positions of the rocks and obstructions in the passage and, apart from NZ615, do you have any other charts or sketches of soundings in the passage?"

"I have no detailed knowledge of the rocks in the passage

other than the fact that when fishing there I have drifted through the passage, fishing in depths estimated at 35 to 40 feet. I have seen no other charts, soundings or drawings until two days ago when a copy of a soundings charts which was drawn up in 1895 was given to me."

"Is that the chart compiled after a survey by T Perham using the New Zealand Government launch named *Pilot* and dated 1894/95?"

"That is the chart I refer to."

Captain Ponsford then asked the pilot to give a detailed description of his attempt to navigate the passage, and the events which followed. Don Jamison said he could not recall any questions about his instructions to the helmsman or his intention to take the ship through the passage being raised by any of the officers on the bridge.[1]

The other crucial question Captain Ponsford asked the pilot was about his consumption of alcohol prior to joining the ship in Picton, and Don Jamison was clear in his answer:

"On arrival on the *Mikhail Lermontov* in Wellington on Saturday 15 February, I met the vessel's agent, Mr T Goss. Mr Goss offered to give myself and the deputy harbourmaster a conducted tour of the vessel. During this tour Mr Goss was called away and asked us to wait for him in the bar. In the bar at the time was the vessel's other agent, Mr Williamson of G H Scales Limited. I purchased a drink for Mr Williamson who had no Australian currency and shortly afterwards an old friend of mine, Mr Ross Dunn, who I met on the wharf, passed through the area with a group of travel agents. He subsequently returned to the bar and had a drink with me. I estimated that within the period of 1530 hours to 1700 hours I would have consumed four cans of lager. That evening Mr Dunn took myself and the deputy harbourmaster to dinner at a Wellington restaurant. I had one gin and tonic before the meal, and with the meal I would have consumed half a bottle of white wine.

---

1. This response was obviously contrary to the testimony of Russian officers on the bridge who clearly in their evidence recalled their anxiety at the sudden change of course through the passage, their questions to the pilot and his assurance that there was nothing to worry about.

On Sunday 16 February, when I attended on board with the harbour board's chairman, we had a small presentation ceremony. I consumed two glasses of vodka and a glass of beer."

"What time would that be?"

"That would be at mid-day or shortly afterwards. I then had lunch on board with the harbour board chairman and the agent, Mr Goss. Three glasses were filled up at each table setting: one glass of vodka, one glass of white wine and one glass of red wine. I drank two glasses of mineral water and left the other glasses untouched."

"When the ship left Picton, apart from your mental and physical impairment, in hindsight were you in full possession of your mental and physical faculties?"

"I considered I was not impaired by any consumption of alcohol. However, again in hindsight, it may have been indicative of my condition in that I would normally never consume alcohol for several hours prior to carrying out a pilotage function and would normally have requested in such circumstances a glass of fruit juice or something similar. By the time we reached the outer pilotage limit I must have been extremely tired although I did not realise it. This probably affected my judgment."

This was the closest any of the officers on board the *Mikhail Lermontov* ever came to suggesting a reason for the loss of the ship. A picture had slowly emerged: an overworked and mentally exhausted pilot had been left on the bridge of the ship after it had passed out of his area of operation. He had not recognised the seriousness of his condition, and had not thought to hand over the control of the ship to a senior officer, or call the master. He then directed the ship through the Cape Jackson Passage without realising the danger that move posed to the 708 people on board.

Two days later, on 26 February, Captain Ponsford wrote his report and recommendations for Transport Minister Richard Prebble. The Minister had already been in contact with Captain Jamison and suggested he should surrender his pilot's licence.

Captain Ponsford's conclusions and recommendation read:

- The *Mikhail Lermontov* grounded in position lat. 40° 59' 36'S Long. 174° 19' 00'E and subsequently sank in position Lat. 41° 03' 30' Long. 174° 12' 30'E.
- The underwater damage to the forepart of the *Mikhail Lermontov* sustained in the grounding was such that the subsequent flooding was more than the ship could sustain and the ship foundered during the attempt to beach the ship at the head of the south-east arm of Port Gore Bay. This was prevented by the ultimate failure of all propulsion power.
- At the time of grounding the ship's course and speed were being directed by Captain D I Jamison in the employ of the Marlborough Harbour Board as harbourmaster and chief pilot.[2]
- At the time of the grounding, the ship's master, Captain Vladislav Vorobyov, was absent from the bridge, and the safe navigation of the ship was the responsibility of the senior deck officer on watch, Mr Sergey Stepanishchev.
- The position in which the ship grounded is in a narrow channel indicated on chart NZ615, the largest-scale chart of the area, to be foul ground.
- The decision to direct the ship through the channel was made by Captain Jamison without consulting any other person at the time the ship was in position Lat. 41° 01' 04' S Long. 174° 19' 30' E.
- Prior to making his decision to direct the ship through the channel, the ship's course was 040° (T), and had that course been maintained, the ship would have safely navigated the area in the vicinity of the grounding.

---

2. This conclusion appears at variance with the uncontested testimony of Captain Jamison who said very clearly he was on leave from his employment with the Marlborough Harbour Board after crossing pilotage limits at Motuara Island, and he had no arrangement with the ship's master to be on the bridge after that time.

The sinking occurred within Marlborough Harbour limits, however, which extend beyond pilotage limits. The conclusion was also to have far-reaching implications for the Marlborough Harbour Board in subsequent litigation.

- Immediately after the grounding, Captain Vorobyov rushed to the bridge, took over the navigation of the ship from Captain Jamison and remained in full control until he himself abandoned ship.
- Following the evacuation of all personnel Captain Vorobyov established that refrigeration engineer Mr Parvee Zagliadimov was missing. Mr Zagliadimov was last seen at approximately 1730 hours on 16 February 1986. At that time Mr Zagliadimov was carrying out his normal duties in or about the refrigerated storerooms and the refrigeration machinery compartment.
- These spaces were on the starboard side forward and in the general area where major damage was sustained on grounding at 1737 hours. It can be assumed that Mr Zagliadimov perished at or soon after 1737 hours on 16 February 1986.
- **Recommendation: As this preliminary enquiry has established, beyond any reasonable doubt, the facts leading to the grounding and subsequent loss of the *Mikhail Lermontov*, it is recommended that no formal investigation be carried out.**

The police had also interviewed the pilot at length and decided there was nothing to be gained by a prosecution, even though there had been a fatality.

It was a view shared by Transport Minister Richard Prebble, who had been informed by the Baltic Shipping Company that they would not co-operate with a full enquiry or a police prosecution. They would hold their own enquiry in Russia.

Only Captain Ponsford's finding and recommendation were released to the public. Individual testimony, more particularly the statement by Don Jamison, was not publicly released.

At a meeting of the Marlborough Harbour Board shortly after the sinking, Don Jamison, accompanied by his lawyer, handed out a written report of his part in the tragedy.

After board members had read the report, all copies were retrieved and handed back to Don Jamison. It was never made public.

Only the naive, however, could have expected the public to accept such a cursory examination of the most dramatic and mysterious shipping loss in the country's maritime history.

CHAPTER TEN

Diving Deep

RAY HATCH knew he was in trouble even before he surfaced. The 36-year-old diver from Kerikeri had been working on the *Mikhail Lermontov*, 90 feet under water in Port Gore, for several hours, and had come up too quickly. He had worked on enough deep diving jobs to know that the uncomfortable feeling in his chest was an early sign of the potentially lethal condition divers know as the bends.

Before he stepped on to the diving tender, *Little Mermaid*, he called for help over his helmet intercom. Then Ray removed his mask while other divers stripped off his dive suit, moving quickly to get him into the decompression chamber.

When divers work for long periods in deep water, the nitrogen from the air they breathe in is absorbed into the blood. There it forms bubbles if someone surfaces too quickly. These bubbles can cause permanent disability in joints, or fatal heart attacks and strokes. To avoid the problem, divers must stop every few metres on the way to the surface, to allow their bodies to adjust to reduced pressure and to exhale the nitrogen. Ray had found it a slow cold process in water which rarely got above 12 degrees. He had come up too quickly.

Suspended underneath the *Little Mermaid*, which had been anchored to the sunken ship to maintain its position, was a special diving bell to give the divers a 'half-way house' where controlled air pressure was used to avoid the problems of rapid surfacing; but using this was also an uncomfortably cold procedure, often taking two or three hours.

There was also a decompression chamber, called 'the bump', on the *Little Mermaid*, which divers used after a quicker surfacing system. They came up faster, with minimal pauses, and were taken immediately to the decompression chamber before gas bubbles had time to form. By being in the increased air pressure inside the chamber, and breathing its pure oxygen, the divers were able to re-adjust to surface pressure in a warm comfortable environment. It was more comfortable and much quicker than using the bell.

Ray Hatch had intended to use the decompression chamber on the *Little Mermaid*, but something had gone wrong with his ascent. He could feel a painful air bubble forming deep in his chest. It was not the first time on a salvage diving operation that he'd been close to trouble; he knew this was serious. He needed help quickly.

Within two days after the ship had gone down, Ray Hatch had been contacted by Ian Lockley, a Fiji-based salvage expert. Ian Lockley was to be salvage master of a joint diving venture to recover safes and other valuables, and to pump oil out of the sunken Soviet liner for the Baltic Shipping Company. The second task was primarily to lessen any environmental disaster, but also to recover a valuable asset.

Ray Hatch was well known in the salvage diving world, so the combined New Zealand and Australian group, which had won the contract against considerable international competition, had wanted him to join them. He'd been happy to do so.

The New Zealand Navy had also sent down a team to investigate the wreck, partly just in case of the extremely remote possibility that any of the far-fetched rumours had any basis whatsoever, and partly for the experience.

Ray Hatch and his diving buddy, Doug Taylor, had been delighted to beat the Navy divers to the ship's bell, the traditional first plunder off a wreck. The trophy had been displayed with a great deal of pride before it was handed over to agents of the ship's owners.

Then they'd got down to the serious side of the operation. Their priority job would be to set up high pressure hoses, enabling the 1,500 tonne of fuel oil on board the ship to be pumped to the surface and into a tanker for removal, before it leaked into the waters of the pristine Marlborough Sounds.

For the first few days they'd been entranced by the rugged beauty of Port Gore. Outside the bay the rough waters of Cook Strait raged and thrashed against Cape Jackson, especially when southerly storms roared in from the Pacific Ocean. Inside the bay they were relatively protected from the worst of the weather, unless it came gusting in from the north-west. Then the bay would be a confusion of white caps and wind-driven spray, making life difficult for the crew on the tender, although surface storms had little effect on the divers working far below the waves.

The water in the bay was as clear as anywhere they had dived, sunlight penetrating for several metres before the deep blue-green gave way to blue-grey and then to the colourless neutrality of deep water.

On the bottom, the huge white form of the ship was a dull glow in the dark surroundings. The Soviet flag and the international pilot's flag still waved slowly in the water from where they were attached from the masthead above the bridge.

Inside, the ship was inky blackness. They could find their way only with powerful lights. If the dust and silt got stirred up, nothing could penetrate the murky interior. Soon the novelty of their surroundings wore off, and they settled down to the long and dangerous job of getting the oil and valuables off the ship.

They had worked steadily for several weeks without mishap before Ray got into trouble. It was now Easter Saturday afternoon and a strong north-west wind was whipping the surface of the water into whitecaps.

After Ray's diving suit had been quickly stripped off and he'd been hurried into the decompression chamber, dive master Rick Poole increased the air pressure until Ray felt the pain subside. He had to be taken to the equivalent of 60 feet, almost two-thirds of the way back to the bottom of Port Gore, before he felt comfortable.

He was low on energy from working in the cold water, and he asked, through the intercom system, if there were any chocolate on board. Some Easter eggs were found and passed in through the airlock system. The air pressure reduced them to shrivelled little brown lumps resembling prunes, but they tasted fine.

After nearly five hours in the chamber Ray was still feeling okay. Rick Poole slowly decreased the pressure, but, when it got to the equivalent of 30 feet, Ray's pain suddenly returned. Rick didn't hesitate. This was a serious situation, and he returned the pressure to the equivalent of 60 feet. The team made an urgent call for the Westpac helicopter in Wellington. Neurosurgeon Russell Worth would come over to try to save the diver's life. He was in imminent danger of becoming the *Mikhail Lermontov's* second victim.

Pilot Ray Button and rescue doctor Russell Worth worked quickly to get the special compression chamber onto the helicopter and get airborne. It was nearly 6pm, with a steadily increasing nor-westerly wind blowing. The rescue team had a bumpy ride across Cook Strait to Port Gore Bay, where they landed near the beach as the light began to fade.

Ray was comfortable only as long as the pressure was kept up. Russell Worth knew there was a dangerous bubble somewhere in Ray's chest which could be removed only by special surgery. He would have to remove it before it found its way into an artery or a vital organ. Ray could die in a few minutes.

Russell Worth joined Ray in the decompression chamber. They discussed the details of the operation. It would have be performed in this chamber: Ray could not be removed safely.

There was little room for the two men plus the equipment needed for the lifesaving procedure. Doctor Worth also had some concern about possible infection. Using a special needle to pierce Ray's side, he attached a tube which was fitted with a one-way valve. This allowed the air inside Ray's chest to escape, but prevented the pressurised air in the chamber from entering.

With Ray now out of immediate danger, the plan was for him to be transferred the next morning to Wellington Hospital, for recovery and observation. The weather on Easter Sunday, however, proved even rougher. The nor-westerly gale increased to 70 knots and the helicopter pilot knew he couldn't fly too high, as the decreased air pressure at a higher altitude could create further complications for Ray.

At a mere 50 feet above a wild, plunging and wind-ravaged Cook Strait, the rescue helicopter raced back to Wellington, arriving just after 7pm. Ray was whisked into hospital. He was very lucky. Two days later he was able to return to the diving team in Port Gore.

He was the first of three divers who suffered an attack of the bends during the 10-month salvage operation. It had been an incident typical of the dangers faced by deepwater salvage divers working for extended periods in extreme conditions.

The dive team had tackled difficult tasks before, but this was the biggest and deepest ship they had worked on, and they had to try to recover the contents of heavy safes as well as recovering the oil.

The engineroom alone could have held a six-storey building, and, with the ship on its side and visibility almost nil, it was easy for even the most experienced diver to lose his sense of direction.

Which way was up or down could be hard to decide. Special guiding ropes were placed, to help the divers find their way back to the outside of the ship if their lights failed. Even with the lights, most divers in the team found visibility so bad that they learned to work in the darkness, with just their sense of touch to guide them, once they had found what they were looking for.

While getting into the safes could require underwater gascutting equipment, the oil posed its own problems. The tanks were under enormous pressure. Special valves would have to be attached when they were breached, and this wasn't going to be at all easy.

They had one important piece of good fortune. A sister ship of the *Mikhail Lermontov*, the *Alexander Pushkin*, also owned by the Baltic Shipping Company, was in New Zealand waters at the time. The dive team was given a guided tour to familiarise themselves with the ship's layout.

Australian Joe Engwirda was in overall charge of the diving. He wanted to map out exactly where and how the divers would penetrate the ship. On the *Alexander Pushkin* they'd carefully examined the skylight covers over the main engineroom, covers which could be opened by removing the retaining pins. Down in the engineroom itself Joe had wanted to see the propeller shaft tunnel, which would give access to some of the oil tanks.

Then, with Malcolm Blair's diving tender, *Little Mermaid*, equipped and ready for the operation, they'd set off from Picton, following almost exactly the track of the *Mikhail Lermontov* a few days before.

They'd known they had to get into the ship quickly before rotting food and soft furnishings made visibility impossible and progress dangerous. Already carpets would be lifting and curtains would be entangling in the underwater currents, forming a deadly trap for inexperienced or unwary divers.

Their first dives had revealed two gashes totalling about 40 feet, nearly 100 feet back from the port bow, where rocks had inflicted their mortal wounds. Any damage to the starboard bow was hidden from view as the ship was lying on that side.

Hundreds of fish had already taken up residence in the ship in the murky depths, blue cod and other bottom-dwellers swimming nonchalantly among the debris below decks.

The ship's clock had stopped at 20 minutes to six. The engineroom telegraph levers were at 'stop engines'. All around was the debris and trash of a shipwreck. The once lavish furnishings were reduced to so much rotting rubbish, even in the few days they had been submerged. Already the ship had begun its rapid process of decay.

At this depth, and under these conditions, the divers had to take every precaution against accidents. They used the most up-to-date diving equipment, including a special deepwater helmet fitted with microphones and speakers for communicating with the dive tender on the surface.

Adding to the communications difficulties, vocal chord distortion was caused by the gases in the mixture they were breathing, and the pressure. Instructions and messages were often difficult to understand. This sophisticated salvage operation required professional skills of the highest level, above and below the surface.

Although they each carried a small scuba tank for emergencies, divers were fed air from a compressor on the tender, through a long 'umbilical' fitted to their helmets, making a direct link with the surface 90 feet above. To maintain their body temperature so they could stay down longer in the near-freezing conditions, hot water was pumped into their suits through a subsection of the umbilical, and a fourth subsection carried a depth reading to the dive controller on the *Little Mermaid*.

Working at this depth required courage, particularly when things did not go according to plan. The umbilical could get snagged while a man was deep inside the ship, and he would have to backtrack carefully, in poor visibility, to free it before carrying on. At other times a face mask would get covered with oil or mud which could not be wiped away. A blind diver is very vulnerable; he would have to explain the situation to the dive controller who would then direct one of the others to go and guide him to safety.

The dive controller, who had the layout of the ship in front of him, knew where each man was. Often the divers did not know their exact location, how deep they were or even how long they had been underwater. Keeping track of all this was the job of the dive controller, leaving the men to concentrate on their complex tasks, such as locating the valves on the oil tanks.

There were tanks in various parts of the ship. Each had to be located, using detailed drawings provided by the Baltic Shipping Company, and prepared for pumping out. Some tanks could be accessed by drilling through the side of the ship with air-driven machinery, and then fitting special pressure valves. Other tanks were deep inside the ship, requiring dangerous internal dives. To gain access to some of them, the special underwater gas cutting equipment was used to open up the side of the ship.

Two months after they began diving on the ship, all the oil tanks had been located and prepared and they were ready to begin pumping. The tanker *Pacific Explorer* arrived to tank the oil, and the final stage of the operation got underway. Fitting the hoses to the tanks was a difficult operation; some had an airpocket which had been compressed to enormous pressure. As it escaped it forced the end of the hose away.

Oil escaping under pressure was even more of a problem, as visibility disappeared immediately the tank was breached. But air-driven and hydraulic pumps were engaged and they were finally 'pumping oil'.

There was still more for the divers to do. Although two safes were to prove impossible to remove, down in the purser's office Ray Hatch located the main safe and attached heavy lines from a lifting bag. When all was ready, air was pumped into the bag, and the heavy safe rose majestically to the surface to be hoisted aboard the dive tender. Back in Picton the safe was opened by Baltic Shipping Company officials, who found the money and papers intact, if somewhat soggy.

Before they left the ship the divers found the cabin belonging to the shore excursions officer, Jean Anderson. She had been at sea for nearly 10 years as an entertainments organiser, and all her worldly goods had gone down with the ship. Inside the cabin the men gathered up as many of her personal possessions as they could find. Among her jewellery were two rings – one from her mother and the other from her husband – which she was particularly delighted to get back. There was also a string of pearls which had turned black from the deep immersion in oily water.

The jewellery was presented to her in front of a film crew who were making a documentary.

Jean Anderson was one of the very few people, apart from the Baltic Shipping Company, to get anything at all back from the wreck.

After living and working from the *Little Mermaid* in Port Gore for three months in all weathers, the diving team finally unshackled their anchor chains from the *Mikhail Lermontov* on the sea floor below them, and headed home.

For a while the Marlborough Harbour Board considered

demanding the removal of the wreck, or removing it themselves and attempting to recover the cost from the Baltic Shipping Company.

But removing the wreck of the ill-fated ferry *Wahine*, which had foundered in shallow water on Barrets Reef near the mouth of Wellington Harbour in 1968, had cost about $NZ10 million. Lifting the *Mikhail Lermontov* from the bottom of Port Gore, either as a complete hull or in sections, would be enormously expensive, and trying to recover the cost from the Soviet Government would be, to say the least, a long shot indeed.

The idea was quickly forgotten. The wreck presented no hazard to shipping, it was now clear of contaminating oil, and the harbour board had other, more pressing, matters to deal with.

Recreational divers from all over New Zealand, Australia and indeed the world very soon saw the possibilities of this new diving site. Word spread rapidly.

One diver with a special interest in it was Jeremy Brew, son of Captain John Brew. He was a reasonably experienced diver when he made the first of his many dives on the *Lermontov* but he felt quite unprepared for what he discovered.

"The sheer size of the thing" struck him forcibly. Visibility was poor so that the cruise ship only gradually loomed out of the murk. "You never get to see the whole ship at once."

Windows had broken along the ship's side so a shallow penetration dive, the first of several, was relatively easy. "You just pop through a window, swim around a bar, a cabin or a shopping area and then simply swim out another window."

Later and deeper penetrations he found far more dangerous. A fine layer of silt covers everything so that the movement of swimming soon reduces visibility to practically nothing. Divers rapidly run out of sunlight as they go deeper into the vessel, and they know disorientation can come quickly in the miles of corridors and stairways. The dangers of this wrecked ship are impressed on every diver. "After all, more people have died on it since it sank than when it originally came to grief."

Jeremy Brew now holds a second mate's ticket. When he is back home in New Zealand between tours of duty on ships in the northern hemisphere he often returns to the *Mikhail Lermontov*. He was asked to recreate a dive.

"My dive buddy Stewart Bagley and I had already done an initial dive exploring the ship together and were now interested in going to some specific spots for a good look. We decided to visit the bridge first.

"We dived down the mooring rope which was attached to the *Lermontov* amidships and swam quickly for'd. A bridge wing window was smashed so we entered there and I went in first, trying not to disturb the silt with my fins. Stewart dropped in after me. The ship is lying on its starboard side so the wheelhouse dropped away at a steep angle below us.

"Once inside we could swim together and explore the bridge. It was pretty much intact and as it was on the night she ran aground. The salvage divers, however, had removed one or two items, including the wheel and the ship's bell, before the ship was opened to recreational divers. I noticed that the radar screen had imploded with the water pressure.

"I indicated to Stu we'd move to the chartroom behind the bridge and moved towards the door. As I went through the narrow corridor I kicked up a little too much silt, and Stu withdrew as he couldn't see.

"Unaware, I continued into the chartroom and started to look through the flag locker and other drawers. This is one of the dangers of wreck living. You can very easily get distracted and lose track of time, your depth or even your air supply. Noticing I hadn't seen Stu, I wriggled around, blinding myself in the silt, and felt for an exit. I figured there would be a way out to the deck from where I was. So, following another corridor, I emerged on the bridgewing to find a very relieved buddy.

"We carried on to look at the damage as planned, before making our slow ascent. We had considered making a deep dive to the engineroom but, after a good deal of thought about the risks, gave it a miss.

"There are several dangers specific to wreck diving. One,

as I've just described, is becoming so engrossed in things a few inches from your face that you don't notice other important things going on around you. Another is being tempted into a dive you can't handle. The deeper part of the dive can give people nitrogen narcosis, causing them to do completely stupid things, which can easily result in death. You don't get away with too many mistakes at 120 feet. Thirdly, with the *Lermontov*, the bulkhead and deckhead linings coming off can cause entrapment problems. A nasty tangle can leave a diver trapped inside the ship."

Jeremy Brew, like virtually every other wreck diver, delighted in finding souvenirs of his dives. His favourites are some commemorative coins, celebrating 150 years of the Baltic Shipping Company. About two and a half inches in diameter, they came in presentation cases and were found in a room just below the bridge, possibly the purser's office.

In spite of, or partly because of, the dangers this wreck presents, it is likely to remain a magnet for divers well into the future.

CHAPTER ELEVEN

A Political Cover-Up?

IT HADN'T TAKEN Richard Prebble long to make up his mind about the *Mikhail Lermontov*. As Minister of Transport in the Labour Government, he knew exactly what he wanted, and the next move after the preliminary enquiry was his.

The facts seemed clear enough. The Soviet cruise ship had hit rocks off Cape Jackson in the Marlborough Sounds, and had gone down in nearby Port Gore with the loss of one life. The Ponsford Preliminary Enquiry into the loss of the ship had recommended that a formal enquiry should not be held, and that suited the minister.

Discussions with the Attorney-General, Geoffrey Palmer, and the Minister of Police, Ann Hercus, also indicated that prosecuting the pilot, Captain Don Jamison, would probably be a waste of time. The Soviets were not interested in co-operating with a New Zealand prosecution, and key witnesses had already returned to the USSR.

Added to all this was an underlying, unyielding fact: trade with the USSR was vital to New Zealand's economy. Securing payment for dairy products already exported was also most important. No government in its right mind would want to fall out with a major trading partner, nor allow any potentially embarrassing situation to drag on. The consensus, undoubtedly, was that the sooner this mess was cleared up, the better.

As to the Marlborough Harbour Board, it was in enough trouble over the dismissal of its general manager, and there were early indications that the board would also be faced with damages claims from both the ship's passengers and its owners. (In a fascinating twist of circumstances, the Marlborough Harbour Board would become the only New Zealand local authority to be sued in an Australian court by the Soviet Government. As there was no challenge to the jurisdiction of the Australian High Court to decide the matter, observers assumed all parties had consented to the arrangement, but even this detail has never been confirmed.)

The board was one of several local authorities which were soon to disappear with the reorganisation of local government throughout New Zealand, and the Transport Minister would be glad to see them go.

New Zealand, as a remote South Pacific nation, was heavily reliant on shipping, but had the slowest ship turn-around ports in the western world. Richard Prebble wanted to see a complete overhaul of the shipping and harbour industries, and getting locally elected politicians out of the way was the first step. His cabinet colleagues agreed, and supported his decision to follow the Ponsford Enquiry recommendation; there would not be a formal investigation.

It was indeed optimistic, however, to expect that the public, the news media, and Opposition politicians would accept that decision without a fuss. Letters to the editors of many newspapers for months demanded full public disclosure of all that was known about the tragedy. Radio talkback shows were in their infancy, but callers wasted little time in loading the airwaves with similar messages.

Some people made genuine enquiries for information on a matter of significant public interest, while others claimed to know all manner of details about the ship. They said they had everything from evidence that all the watertight doors had been left open, to bombs having exploded on board. Most of these people were refugees from the lunatic fringe. Links with unidentified flying objects, and complex undercover theories, were almost as common as they were far-fetched.

Political questions in New Zealand were not as easily dismissed. Richard Prebble was on his feet many times over the next year, fielding searching enquiries about the loss of the ship. His main antagonist was the ambitious National MP for Tauranga, Winston Peters, who never missed an opportunity to ask about the *Mikhail Lermontov*.

Peters, showing an early appetite for conspiracy theories, was also happy to use as ammunition the sinking of the Greenpeace flagship, *Rainbow Warrior*. She had been sunk at her moorings in the early hours of 10 July 1985, in Auckland, by French undercover agents using limpet mines. This had followed high profile local protests against nuclear tests in the Pacific. Winston Peters didn't think highly of the way the Labour Government had handled either event.

At the end of May 1986, during question time in Parliament, it became obvious that some details about the watertight doors in the *Mikhail Lermontov* had been revealed. Winston Peters asked: "Did the New Zealand naval divers looking for the body of the missing engineer from the *Mikhail Lermontov* observe the state of the watertight doors in the ship; if so, were they found to be open or closed, and why?"

Richard Prebble was absent, but had left a prepared answer with Works and Development Minister Fraser Coleman who replied: "The Royal New Zealand Navy divers who were engaged in searching for the body of the missing crewman on the *Mikhail Lermontov* did report that two watertight doors were open. They were located in two of the watertight bulkheads forward of the machinery spaces.

"One can only speculate at this stage about why the doors were open, although I have no doubt that the Soviet authorities will enquire closely into the matter.

"There are several possible explanations, the most likely being that, after the initial closure of all the 28 watertight doors in the ship by remote operation from the bridge, the two doors in question were subsequently opened, using local control, by damage control parties or people searching for the missing crewman.

"Four watertight compartments forward of the machinery spaces were flooded and left open to the sea, so the fact that those two doors were left open would probably have made little difference to the extent or rate of flooding of those compartments."

Such detailed information could have come only from the unpublished files of the Ponsford Enquiry. Winston Peters asked: "Was the information in the answer the Minister has just given derived from the findings and evidence before the Preliminary Enquiry?"

Fraser Coleman was not about to be drawn out so easily. "I imagine that the information I have conveyed from the Minister of Transport was obtained as a result of what the naval divers found when they inspected the ship," he said.

New Zealand and Australian newspapers gleaned what information they could from those involved in the tragedy who were prepared or authorised to speak openly, but key figures remained tight-lipped.

The most comprehensive news coverage came from Television New Zealand's Carol de Colville who undertook a thorough investigation of the tragedy and its aftermath. Central to her two-part television programme on the loss of the ship were two experienced master mariners. They were openly critical of the Government's handling of the affair.

The former commander of the New Zealand Navy ships *Waikato* and *Otago*, Ian Bradley, and the deputy harbourmaster of Timaru, Captain Ian Cook, were both adamant that there should have been a full enquiry into the sinking, and that the Russian senior officers should have been called to account.

As it happened, Ian Cook's immediate superior, Timaru harbourmaster Brian Petrie, was one of the three-man tribunal to hear an action for unjustified dismissal brought against the Marlborough Harbour Board by Don Jamison's immediate superior, Mike Goulden. Brian Petrie was the only member of the tribunal to vote in favour of the harbour board.

Ian Bradley in particular was convinced there had been some sort of official cover-up. He was especially concerned that the Ponsford Enquiry had found the ship had struck on the starboard side, but divers had found large gashes in her port side. The television programme showed him returning from a dive on the ship to confirm there were holes in the port side. He could not see the starboard side as the ship was lying over that way. It was incomprehensible, he said, that any experienced seaman would deliberately take a large ship through the Cape Jackson Passage.

Ian Cook was concerned that Don Jamison had been made to take all the blame for the loss of the ship without a full enquiry, and that the Russians had not been criticised, much less charged with an offence, by New Zealand authorities.

Carol de Colville questioned both the Transport Minister, Richard Prebble, and the Director of Marine, Hugh Jones, at length on the apparent need for a full public enquiry, but to no avail. Hugh Jones said he had approved the Ponsford Report, which had recommended that no further action should be taken, before it went to Richard Prebble for final acceptance. He flatly refused to be drawn into a debate on his own personal views on the matter.

Richard Prebble was typically scathing of the two seamen who had criticised his handling of the tragedy. He said the pubs were full of retired master mariners who wanted further enquiries into every shipping disaster since the *Marie Celeste*.

He said he had no authority to take any action against the Russian seamen, and any action against Don Jamison would have been a farce as the Russians had said they would not return to New Zealand for a trial, or co-operate in any way.

One particularly dramatic scene in Carol de Colville's news programme showed Picton boatyard operator Peter McManaway pulling rotten lifejackets from the *Mikhail Lermontov* apart with his hands. He said he found some of the lifeboats to be in sub-standard order. They had holes, from leaked battery acid, through the alloy hull, and one had a disconnected exhaust pipe from an engine. He also said he had found holed and empty drinking water containers, and rotten timber.

Peter McManaway said he had no doubt that hundreds of lives would have been lost if the *Mikhail Lermontov* had sunk farther out to sea.

The Ponsford Enquiry, however, had found lifesaving equipment to be in good order. Who was correct? Carol de Colville's questions to officials about the obvious contradictions were simply ignored.

Other sections of the news media were far less professional in their reporting of the event. One Fleet Street tabloid exceeded all others in shoddy journalism. Reporter Rafe Klinger may have heard about the first boat which had been seen to go towards the shore, the boat which had been sent to check how suitable it would be for unloading passengers. As darkness thickened and general small-boat activity around the ship increased, the boat was not seen returning, although in fact it did so by way of the *Tarihiko*, where it transferred its passengers.

Or perhaps the germ from which the tabloid's diatribe sprang was the incident involving the lifeboat full of Russian crew members, which had been heading for Picton before being turned back to the *Arahura* by *HMNZS Taupo*. Whatever the source and without checking it out, in a sensational and glaringly inaccurate piece entitled 'Chickens of the Sea', Klinger wrote:

"In one of the most shameful incidents in the history of the seven seas, yellow belly Russian sailors deserted their sinking ship like slimy rats leaving hundreds of helpless passengers to face certain death in the cruel dark waters.

"Luckily, a New Zealand Navy patrol boat happened by, forcing the cowardly Russian seamen to return and help rescue the passengers.

"Only one of the 737 passengers and crew of the ill-fated Soviet cruise ship *Mikhail Lermontov* was lost – no thanks to the craven crew members.

"Lt Peter Batchelor, an officer on board the New Zealand vessel, described the disgraceful scene when his boat encountered the fleeing Russian sailors.

"Lt Batchelor said the Russian seaman had actually packed their bags before slinking on board modern motorised lifeboats without even alerting passengers that the ship was sinking. 'Passengers had to realise for themselves that something was going wrong,' he testified at an enquiry in Wellington, New Zealand.

"'Many lifeboats were so rotten that passengers holed them with their feet. Many of the inflatable liferafts would not open and those that we picked up were leaking so badly after the disaster that they were sinking.'

"Rescue lights on the liferafts weren't working and passenger after passenger said no alarm had been given. Even worse, many of the passengers on board the 22,000-ton Soviet ship were elderly persons who had little or no chance of surviving a long ordeal of drifting in the ocean in leaky lifeboats.

"Luckily the ship was not far from New Zealand's South Island when it struck rocks which pierced its steel hull. The *Mikhail Lermontov* sank in 108 feet of water. Even worse than the cowardly escape by the Russian crew was the way the Russian captain explained the tragic accident. Captain Vladislav Vorobyov denied responsibility for the disaster, claiming that a New Zealand pilot stupidly steered his ship to the metal-mangling rocks."

With news stories so ridiculously inaccurate appearing in newspapers on the other side of the world from the event, it was little wonder there was confusion about what really happened. Russian authorities could also be excused for not wanting to talk to journalists of any nation.

Back in Parliament, however, Opposition MP Winston Peters was not about to let the Marlborough Harbour Board and the Transport Minister off as easily as that. He wanted to know more about the lost ship. "If, as the Minister said in answer to an earlier question and in a press release, he had reached his decision not to hold a formal enquiry into the loss of the *Mikhail Lermontov* without consultation with the owners of the ship, is that normal practice?"

Mr Prebble was equal to the occasion. He said he could consult or not consult almost with anyone he chose. "I may take account of the recommendation of the Preliminary Enquiry, and of any other factors or information available to me, but it is not usual to consult the owners of the ship, or ships involved."

Winston Peters saw an opening to inflict further discomfort, and pounced. "If that is true, and I refer to the Minister's original answer, why did he say on Thursday March 6: 'Having read the report, having personally read much of the evidence given to the enquiry, and having discussed the matter with the *Mikhail Lermontov's* owners' – something he denied the other day – 'I have accepted the recommendation and there will be no formal enquiry?'"

Other Members of Parliament sat back to watch the encounter with interest and enjoyment. Richard Prebble was a street fighter, a politician who recognised few equals and no superiors. Over the years he had crossed verbal swords with the best the National Party had to field, including the often brutal Rob Muldoon, and he had rarely left the debating chamber in defeat.

Winston Peters had also come up through a hard political school. He didn't enter an arena without being well armed with ammunition. He was reputed to have never asked a question he did not already know the answer to, and was not easily side-stepped. If one man was a battleaxe, the other was a fencing foil, and the debating chamber was their battlefield.

Richard Prebble was not one to shrink from verbal brawls inside or outside Parliament, and now counter-punched the accusation.

"If the Member had listened to my answer he would not make incorrect allegations in his question. There is no requirement in the Act for me to consult the owners of any vessel.

"In this case I did discuss the issue with the owners because, first, as the ship is a foreign vessel there is some interest in the matter of whether there would be an enquiry in the Soviet Union; and, secondly – a matter that may have escaped the Member – if the owners did not want to have an enquiry in this country there is no law or power open to me to require any citizen to attend such an enquiry, and it would be a total sham."

Peter Dunne raced to his rescue with another question, to get the obvious answer: "Is the Minister satisfied that the correct procedures have been followed?"

Richard Prebble assured the House that no representations had been made, and no evidence submitted to him, to suggest that the course of action he had followed had been anything other than legally correct and the only course open to him.

Mr Peters wanted to know why the Transport Minister had not been completely consistent in his responses: "Which is true, the press statement or the reply to my question?"

Richard Prebble stepped back from the fray and blandly said, "Both statements are correct."

Mr Peters was not done yet; he thought he had his man on the ropes. "Does that mean that the press statement made at 3pm on Thursday March 6, when the Minister said, 'and having discussed the matter with the *Mikhail Lermontov's* owners' – a condition precedent to the answer – 'I have decided to accept the recommendation, and there will be no formal enquiry,' was a false statement?"

Mr Prebble was now cornered and tried to retreat further out of trouble by saying he could still see no conflict. Winston Peters closed on his opponent. "How does the Minister square the third paragraph of the press statement of March 6 with the statement, 'the ship owners were not consulted prior to my decision not to order a formal investigation'?"

The Transport Minister had had enough by this time and simply said he could still not see any conflict, refusing to be drawn further. The debate had reached an obvious stalemate. The Speaker would not accept a further question on the subject.

It was one of several such encounters over the months following the loss of the ship. Try as they might, the National Party Opposition never managed to get an admission from Richard Prebble that he had covered up anything in the tragedy. No formal enquiry was ever held.

As far as the public was concerned, to all intents and purposes the Prime Minister, David Lange, did not become embroiled in the situation. He left the matter to his Minister of Transport.

Some time later, however, he did utter a typical Lange-quip:

"Since World War Two, New Zealand is the only country in the western world to have sunk a Russian ship."

CHAPTER TWELVE
Death Throes of a Harbour Board

AS in a Greek tragedy, the seeds of the *Mikhail Lermontov* disaster had been sown much earlier.

Three men, none most notable for humility, flexibility or ability to work co-operatively, held centre stage. They were Marlborough Harbour Board chairman Bruno Dalliessi and the board's harbourmaster and pilot, Don Jamison, standing shoulder to shoulder on the one side, and the board's general manager, Mike Goulden, on the other.

The trouble had begun years before, but by and large had been hushed up.

Now the Marlborough Harbour Board could no longer keep the lid on what had previously been its relatively unknown inner turmoil.

It was obvious to the news media and to the government that the board was well out of its depth, in political and financial trouble over the loss of the ship as well as over the now very public and messy squabble with its former general manager, Mike Goulden. He had just won an Appeal Board decision against his second dismissal from the harbour board.

The High Court had earlier directed the board to reconsider its 1984 decision to dismiss Mike Goulden. It did this five months later – only to dismiss him again. Mike Goulden had then taken the matter to a special Appeal Board, which was in the process of hearing the case when the *Mikhail Lermontov* went down.

Even in his first role as assistant general manager, Mike Goulden and his style of management had not been popular with some elected board members who did not like losing direct financial control. It had taken a year for things to come to a head but, by then, sides had been clearly drawn between two camps within the board: those who supported Mike

Goulden's appointment and his style of management, and those who wanted to retain the old system with Captain Jamison as head of staff.

The conflict had created a difficult working environment which had taken its toll of most people concerned, including senior staff who tried not to get caught up in the conflict. Earlier, just 13 months after Mike Goulden's appointment to the general manager's position, the then board chairman, Harry Stace, had finally run out of patience with the bickering between some board members and senior staff.

At the next board meeting he had let members know he expected them to abide by majority decisions and stop fuelling the dispute which had developed between the general manager and the harbourmaster. In particular he singled out one board member, Bruno Dalliessi, whom he accused of creating similar problems for the previous general manager, Alan Crawley. Mr Stace told the board the general manager was being undermined and sniped at almost continuously, and he expected that sort of behaviour to stop.

The board had entered a new era of commercial operations. The old days of members running the business of the board had gone, but some members, and one in particular, had not accepted the changes made by proper majority decision, he said. The normally quiet-spoken and gentle-mannered chairman was thoroughly angry, and was determined to protect his manager from further harassment.

"During recent months and weeks there has been a string of interferences that have taken up many hours of time that would have been better spent in productive work for the board. Mr Dalliessi, you are that board member. You have no loyalty to the board or its administration. You have never fully accepted the board's majority decision to appoint Mr Goulden as general manager. Last year you accused him of taking leave to which he was not entitled and ultimately, in committee, had to apologise to him," Mr Stace said.

It was a stinging rebuke, delivered in a public meeting, but it had little effect in healing the rift between Bruno Dalliessi and harbourmaster Don Jamison on the one side, and general manager Mike Goulden on the other. It did however bring the dispute into the public arena just prior to the 1980 local body elections which followed.

The public had grown weary of the harbour squabble by this time, and Bruno Dalliessi (standing in the Picton ward) lost his seat on the Marlborough Harbour Board, but did not give up his campaign to regain control. He was well used to the rough and tumble of local politics. He was a former mayor of Picton, and had stood unsuccessfully for Parliament in 1972. He was also well known as having been a national heavyweight boxing champion in his youth, and as a local publican.

With Bruno Dalliessi gone from the board, newly-elected Picton ward member Bill Horrey, a real estate agent, was elected to the chairmanship. Mike Goulden was able to settle down and develop a number of commercial initiatives. Although cautious at first, Bill Horrey, who was well aware of past conflicts, quickly established a good professional working relationship with the manager.

Bill Horrey was aware of the need to separate the political and professional functions of the board, and he was determined to get the operation back on an even keel. Berthing marinas in Picton harbour and nearby Waikawa Bay were upgraded, and work on an extensive management plan for the Marlborough Sounds was started.

The harbour board also doubled as the Marlborough Sounds Maritime Planning Authority, with responsibilities for allocating areas for the newly established marine farming industry and other commercial and recreational activities. The region had also been extensively planted in radiata pine forests, and logging posed its own particular problems for the delicate Sounds environment.

The board had become a much more busy place, but Mike Goulden and Don Jamison had never settled their differences. The uneasy peace was not to last. Three years later, in 1983, Bruno Dalliessi (this time standing in the Blenheim ward in the local body elections), was back on the board. He had run an intensive election campaign.

He wasted no time getting to grips with his old foe Mike Goulden. Before the elections he had promised to "bring the staff to heel," and give the board new direction.

There had been a suggestion that the harbour board had taken out a loan with local residents' private homes as security. Although eventually found to be entirely false, this rumour had been enough to unseat real estate agent Bill Horrey, and return Bruno Dalliessi to the board.

He won the support of the majority of board members who, like him, missed the old style of running the operation from the boardroom and having a staff who did as they were told.

Bruno Dalliessi was elected as chairman at the first meeting and, at the conclusion of general business, all staff members were asked to leave. Then the new chairman and his supporters tabled a list of complaints about the general manager's performance. They demanded more information from Mike Goulden about what he was doing. They now wanted to be more closely involved in the management of the board's affairs, they said.

Within three months the board had accused the general manager of not co-operating with the chairman, and warned him he would be fired if there was no improvement.

Graham Fuller, whose background was insurance, company secretarial and sharebroking, had been a member of the Marlborough Harbour Board for nine years. Under the previous chairman, Bill Horrey, he had been deputy chairman.

He had assessed the professional managerial style of the board's general manager, Mike Goulden, and observed that he was "the driving force" in the board's work. This included pushing along the planning for the board's very considerable marina at Waikawa, the largest in the South Island, and the purchase of more land in Shakespeare Bay.

Fuller, more accustomed than other board members were to the distinction between the powers and activities of directors and chief executives, was the acknowledged spokesman for those board members who took a different stance from Bruno Dalliessi on many matters.

Together with board members Tom Eckford, a retired

mariner, and Dinny Cambridge, a retired farmer, Graham Fuller frequently warned the board that they were going too far.

"We three said all along to the board that the sacking of Mike Goulden, on the evidence they had, was not justified, and that they were allowing their personal feelings to override their good judgement."

Court judgements were later to agree.

But a showdown was inevitable. It came just a year later when Bruno Dalliessi presented a report to the board on the general manager's performance. Headed "Performance Relating to the Withholding of Information from Dalliessi", the report was more than an accusation about withheld information. It was a general and damning criticism of Mike Goulden's overall performance. The general manager was summoned to a special board meeting to answer the allegations.

Mike Goulden was given only 24 hours to read the report. He attended the meeting with his lawyer, who suggested that, as the report had been written by Bruno Dalliessi, he should stand down from the chairmanship while the report was considered. The suggestion was refused. Mike Goulden and his lawyer spent some time responding to the allegation of non-co-operation, then retired while the board considered his fate.

No record was kept of the board's deliberations and even the tape recorder, which was normally used to assist the minute secretary to record meetings, was turned off. At the end of the meeting it was no surprise to anyone when the board decided, with nine votes to three, to dismiss the general manager. He could take three months' special leave on full pay, then his employment would be terminated.

Like Bruno Dalliessi, however, Mike Goulden was a fighter, but from a different school. He had been in the British Army, had been a detective in London and had later led three UN missions in the Middle East and one to the Pakistan Indian border. In New Zealand he had worked as a detective, later working for a number of government department head offices in Wellington before joining the harbour board.

He was no stranger to conflict or difficult situations, and was not about to be intimidated or to have his professional reputation ruined by small town politicians. He knew the legal system as well as many lawyers, having partially completed a law degree. He appealed his dismissal to the High Court.

Chief Justice Sir Ronald Davison found the dismissal had been unfair, as the board had been biased and they had prejudged the case. Sir Ronald commented on Bruno Dalliessi's well known dislike of Mike Goulden, and his willingness to accept last-minute accusations against the general manager without giving him adequate time to respond.

The other eight board members who supported the dismissal were also found to have prejudged the general manager, Sir Ronald said in his decision. He set aside Mike Goulden's dismissal and instructed the harbour board to reconsider the matter.

The board waited five months to put the matter on the agenda and then considered 600 pages of new and detailed accusations against the general manager. After three days' deliberation the board sacked him again.

Mike Goulden was also prepared for a long battle and appealed against his second dismissal. A three-man Appeal Board headed by District Court Judge Michael Hobbs, assisted by Brian McClelland QC, and Timaru Harbour Board chairman Brian Petrie, was set up to consider the complex and bitter squabble which had now not only divided the harbour board but the Marlborough community as well. People from all walks of life took sides in the fight, without knowing many of the details, but with strong opinions nonetheless.

During the third week of the Appeal Board hearings, Bruno Dalliessi and three of his supporters on the board presented new allegations against Mike Goulden. The four board members had also made a formal complaint to the police, accusing the general manager of fraud and false overseas travel expense claims.

They had kept the new allegations to themselves and sought full board approval to present the accusations to the Appeal

Board only the day before they were to be heard. Initially the Appeal Board did not want to hear the new charges against the general manager, but agreed, after being persuaded, that they were very serious.

It did not take long for the Appeal Board to establish that the new charges did not have any factual foundation. This embarrassed the board's lawyer, who quickly asked for them to be withdrawn. The Appeal Board refused this request, preferring the charges to remain on the record as an indication of the majority of the harbour board members' actions.

On 5 June 1986, four months after the loss of the *Mikhail Lermontov*, the Appeal Board finally delivered its decision in favour of Mike Goulden, and fired a scathing broadside at nine members of the harbour board and Captain Jamison for their part in the affair.

It was the majority opinion of the Appeal Board that Captain Jamison held Mike Goulden responsible for the changes to the harbour board's structure and operations, and wanted the new general manager out of the way.

"Captain Jamison was almost obsessional in his belief that no-one should interfere with his authority as harbourmaster and his domain in general," the Appeal Board's decision read.

The Appeal Board also said the extent of Captain Jamison's dislike of Mike Goulden was obvious from the contents of his confidential report on the general manager's performance. "We are satisfied he played no small part in agitating for Mr Goulden's removal," the Appeal Board wrote, and went on to comment on the harbour board's decision to confirm Captain Jamison's position as harbourmaster, a decision taken soon after the *Mikhail Lermontov* went down.

"We find this remarkable, and in our opinion it is some indication of a desire on the part of Mr Dalliessi and a majority of the board to present a united front in support of Captain Jamison in opposition to Mr Goulden."

While the Appeal Board's comments about Captain Jamison's actions were harsh, they were mild compared with those levelled at Bruno Dalliessi and his eight supporters on the harbour board. Judge Hobbs and Brian McClelland said the nine board members' actions in trying to dismiss the general manager had been deplorable and inexcusable.

The third member of the Appeal Board, Brian Petrie, who had voted in support of the dismissals, said Mike Goulden was unsuitable for such a position of authority over so many people, because the general manager was arrogant and insensitive. Even Brian Petrie, however, said the actions of the nine Marlborough Harbour Board members had been "scurrilous and vindictive".

Although both the High Court and the Appeal Board had found in favour of Mike Goulden, it was clear he could not return to his position as general manager of the harbour board while Bruno Dalliessi and his supporters were still in office, and Transport Minister Richard Prebble was determined not to remove them – just yet. That left the board and its general manager to negotiate a settlement. Mike Goulden had incurred thousands of dollars in legal expenses protecting his name, and lost a further considerable sum in salary. He took out civil claims against the board and the chairman to recover the lot.

Five days after the Appeal Board decision, during oral question time, the Labour MP for Ohariu, Peter Dunne, attempted to relieve the political pressure by asking questions that would show the Marlborough Harbour Board was the master of its own, uncertain, destiny. He asked if his colleague the Minister of Transport had any powers to intervene in the affairs of the board, knowing full well he did not.

It was the last thing both MPs wanted and Richard Prebble took the obviously pre-arranged opportunity: "In respect of the recent Appeal Board decision I am advised that as Minister of Transport I have no explicit power to intervene in the affairs of the Marlborough Harbour Board unless special legislation is enacted. The matter involves complex legal issues, and I have asked my officials to examine it further.

"The Appeal Board decision reveals that serious allegations have been made about the possible mishandling of public money. The Auditor-General has been appointed by Parliament to have statutory oversight of all public money. I have accordingly referred to the Auditor-General's office a copy of the Appeal Board's decision, for him to review it and consider whether there has been a misuse of public money, and, if there has been, to take whatever action he thinks is appropriate."

To sheet home the separation and leave the ball firmly in the Marlborough Harbour Board's court, Peter Dunne then asked: "Can the Minister elaborate on the first part of his answer, particularly in relation to the action he is taking with officials at the moment?"

Richard Prebble again took the cue: "I have asked my officials to take up the matter that has been publicly stated by members of the Marlborough Harbour Board, namely, that they would like a commission to be set up. I have formally written to the Marlborough Harbour Board asking if that is the view of all board members. I understand that they will have a meeting tomorrow at which, I imagine, the matter will be canvassed," he said.

If his arch-rival Winston Peters was not impressed or convinced by the Minister's reply, the capital city's morning newspaper, *The Dominion*, was even less so. The paper's editorial for the day, 19 June, suggested that the voters of Marlborough should do something about the Marlborough Harbour Board even if Transport Minister Richard Prebble would not. The editorial, under the title 'Board In Big Trouble', read:

"Marlborough Harbour Board chairman Bruno Dalliessi says he does not see any problems in mending the board's broken bridges. It is impossible to see what evidence would allow him to express such extraordinary optimism. From the Appeal Board's decision it is clear that bitter personality clashes were behind the unjustified sacking of former general manager Mike Goulden. Twenty months of legal wrangling can not have smoothed the path to reconciliation.

"But it is the board itself which surely poses the major problem. A majority of the elected members persisted with flimsy allegations against Mr Goulden, now found to be unsustainable. The board has spent somewhere between

$150,000 and $250,000 pursuing its case. The price has been high in human terms. Within the local economy the effect on promotional and investment efforts has angered the business community.

"It is now difficult to believe that the people who elected the board, let alone those who have to deal directly with it, could continue to have confidence in its judgment. In October the local body elections will provide an opportunity for the public to express any dissatisfaction, and efforts are being made locally to promote new candidates. But Transport Minister Richard Prebble must consider seriously whether the matter can wait four months.

"There is a good case for him to suspend the board and replace it with a commissioner. One of the few board members to support Mr Goulden over the past 20 months, Mr Graham Fuller, has recommended this action.

"Meantime the Appeal Board's decision confirms yet again that Mr Prebble has seriously erred in not ordering a formal enquiry into the sinking of the *Mikhail Lermontov*. The board's harbourmaster and acting general manager, Captain Don Jamison, was the pilot of the *Mikhail Lermontov* when it foundered. Some five weeks later the board confirmed Captain Jamison in his position as harbourmaster. 'We are bound to say that in all the circumstances we find this remarkable,' the Appeal Board stated.

"A preliminary investigation showed Captain Jamison ordered a change of course that led to the grounding. It was a sudden decision made without consultation. Though Captain Jamison surrendered his pilot's licence, the reason for his decision has never been made public.

"Other serious issues also remain unexplained. The ship's safety equipment was suspect; evacuation procedures were criticised; and no emergency signal was sent from the ship.

"A full enquiry would clarify these damaging issues and lead to a re-examination of procedures. This is important if New Zealand is to have the full confidence of international shipping interests in piloting and other safety procedures.

"The Soviet Union took the shipwreck sufficiently seriously

to hold an enquiry and prompt action according to very demanding standards. By contrast Mr Prebble has been lax in this matter. He has been satisfied to let it rest with an entirely unsatisfactory preliminary enquiry that left questions with serious implications unanswered.

"The Appeal Board's judgment provides an opportunity for Mr Prebble to rectify his misjudgment. He should grasp it."

Officials from the Auditor-General's Office called on the Marlborough Harbour Board, following the questions in Parliament, to investigate the alleged misappropriation of board money by Mike Goulden. They found nothing out of place.

Eventually the board had to accept defeat. It paid Mike Goulden $624,000 which, added to the board's own legal expenses of $215,000 in the brutal and unnecessary fight, was just over one-third of the board's operating profits for 1987. The Goulden Affair, as it became known, was, like the details of the sinking of the *Mikhail Lermontov*, also kept under close wraps until it was finally concluded.

The Marlborough Express, the normally mild-mannered daily newspaper for the region, was scathing in its editorial on the final settlement. The paper had followed the saga closely in spite of efforts by the board to keep details from publication.

The newspaper's editorial for Tuesday 15 December 1987, entitled 'The Goulden Affair', read:

"There will be sighs of relief that the lengthy dispute between the general manager of the Marlborough Harbour Board, Mr Mike Goulden, and the board has been finally settled, even though at enormous cost.

"Little more than a century ago disagreements of that nature would have been settled with pistols at dawn. People would frown on such solutions today, preferring instead to rely on costly, time-consuming litigation in the courts. While the crack of pistols brought matters to a swift and untimely end for one or both of the adversaries, justice rarely was ever done.

"Unfortunately little has changed even with a just and

objective legal system. Mr Goulden's complete vindication notwithstanding, events proved it was only a matter of time before he was offered a substantial settlement to retire gracefully. Dispensing with his services has been achieved at substantial cost in public money.

"Mr Goulden brought a high standard of professionalism to the board administration, but it appears his style and manner did not go down with some board and staff members, and outsiders. So it was decided to dismiss him. But the board went about the dismissal procedure in a clumsy, ham-fisted manner that later was to earn the scorn of the courts and a special tribunal. Employers can follow well-defined procedures in terminating the jobs of staff they claim do not measure up. Unfortunately, the previous board displayed a sad lack of professionalism and industrial relations expertise in dealing with the matter, with the result it ended up with egg on its collective face.

"The original dispute faded into insignificance as individuals and factions stuck rigidly to predetermined conclusions and ensured the controversy dragged on. Now it is settled, one questions whether the public interest is best served by a group of laymen board members adjudicating on the expenditure of extravagant sums of public money, to extricate them from a calamity of their own making."

The board, however, remained unrepentant. It refused to make public acknowledgement of any fault or misconduct.

CHAPTER THIRTEEN
Final Moves

MOST Marlborough local body politicians had kept out of the bitter disputes which had become a feature of the Marlborough Harbour Board since the appointment of Mike Goulden as general manager. With a population of fewer than 40,000 people, the largely rural province had civic leaders who were known to each other. Many were personal friends. Most had also developed entrenched opinions on the rights and wrongs of the protracted battles which had split the tiny Picton township and fuelled endless conjecture throughout Marlborough.

In the clubs, pubs and sporting venues where local politicians met and mingled with their constituents, however, there had developed an unspoken understanding that the harbour board's troubles were not openly discussed. It was something akin to the traditional prohibition on discussing religion and politics in some social clubs. Even if they had wanted to discuss the board's problems, most local politicians, including a number of harbour board members themselves, were as uninformed as the public.

After the loss of the *Mikhail Lermontov*, the board's legal battles took on a new and worrying complexion. Wrongfully sacking a general manager and stubbornly refusing to reinstate him was one thing. Having the local pilot sink a Soviet luxury passenger liner in home waters was another matter entirely. A number of local authority members were now seriously concerned that the assets of the board, including the new port company – which were all the communal property of ratepayers – could be at risk in the legal battles unfolding in Australia.

In 1988, two years after the sinking, the New Zealand Government had introduced a new system of local government which required the Marlborough Harbour Board to be divided in two: a commercial arm to operate the lucrative Cook Strait

Rail Ferry Terminal in Picton and marina berths and similar services, and a regulatory body to administer marine farm licences and regulate maritime developments in the Marlborough Sounds.

Later the board's regulatory functions, as with all New Zealand's harbour boards, were to be transferred to new local authorities and the boards were to be abolished. Other changes included the abolition of borough councils and a host of single-purpose local authorities which had evolved over the years but had largely become outdated and too cumbersome in a world of computer-based international communication and commerce. They were replaced with larger district and regional councils with a new system of governance based on the separation between policy development and professional management.

In Marlborough the new regional council would eventually own the major portion of new port company shares, with a smaller portion going to the neighbouring Kaikoura District Council. To ensure a smooth change-over to the new system in each region, transitional councils had been established.

So that the new local authorities would not inherit any legal liabilities associated with the loss of the *Mikhail Lermontov*, however, the Marlborough Harbour Board was allowed to remain in operation until all litigation was concluded. In Marlborough there were now open discussions about the consequences for the whole community if litigation in the Australian High Court went against the board.

In Australia a group of 151 passengers, headed by Joan Dillon as a "representative case", had brought a class action in the Supreme Court against the charterers of the *Mikhail Lermontov*, CTC Cruises, and the Baltic Shipping Company, for the loss of their personal belongings and their holiday cruise.

The company had reimbursed passengers for the A$1006.35 "unused" portion of their A$2715 fares but the passengers were seeking much more than that. Mrs Dillon had claimed between A$83,000 and A$108,600 in total damages.

Her lawyer, Peter King, used the recent pleasure boat disaster on the River Thames in England, in which people had been trapped underneath their boat, as a precedent for his client's claim. He told Judge Kenneth Curruthers it was absurd to suggest people caught in that position did not suffer.

"No matter how good a swimmer you are, there is no escape. That was Mrs Dillon's position until just before the ship sank," he said.

He claimed compensation for the loss of enjoyment of the cruise, assessed at ten times the cost of the ticket. This was based on the English court's having awarded damages of twice the cost of the Thames River holiday, which had none of the *Mikhail Lermontov's* "horrific" circumstances: holding on to a rope for 90 minutes to stay upright in the listing ship, sliding down a rope ladder and then falling about two metres into a rescue boat ten minutes before the ship sank.

It was first-class courtroom theatre, and the press gallery was impressed even if the judge appeared unmoved. Mr King now warmed to his subject. He outlined the effects on Mrs Dillon such as nervous shock, bruising, "massive headaches" and constant pain in the neck and shoulders which limited her ability to do her housework. The list of long-term effects on the passengers, most of whom were elderly, took some time to read to the court.

When Mr King finally sat down, lawyers for CTC Cruises and the Baltic Shipping Company were in no doubt their clients were facing a difficult claim to defend.

A smaller group of 38 passengers also filed an action against Pilot Don Jamison for NZ$132,000.

Captain Jamison, through his lawyers, initially challenged the jurisdiction of the Australian Supreme Court to hear an action brought against him, a New Zealand citizen, by the Soviet Government. He later withdrew the challenge, saying he had "decided not to participate in proceedings".

Had he participated in the case, or had the hearings been in a New Zealand court, there was no doubt he would have been asked a great many more searching questions than those he had faced during the Ponsford Enquiry, and it would have been in open court.

Journalists in both Australia and New Zealand looked forward to the day Don Jamison, the key figure in the loss of the *Mikhail Lermontov*, would be forced to give evidence under oath. A number of lawyers also anticipated the opportunity to cross-examine the pilot.

But Don Jamison was determined never to speak in public about the loss of the ship, and has yet to do so. The question of jurisdiction was never raised again, and remains unanswered.

The Baltic Shipping Company and CTC Cruises, anticipating the failure of their defence in court, then filed a cross- claim against the Marlborough Harbour Board and Don Jamison for NZ$197,000. If the claims succeeded, there was no doubt other claims for similar amounts for each of the passengers would follow. With a limit of NZ$5 million in public liability insurance, the board was in serious trouble if all claims against it were successful.

It was shaping up to be a protracted, complex and fascinating case, but the board still appeared, at least to the public, confident of the outcome.

Then the New South Wales Supreme Court lowered the boom on the beleaguered board. In April 1989 Judge Curruthers allowed the ship's owners to increase their cross-claim against the board and its pilot to include the value of the ship.This had been estimated at about NZ$25 million.

Here was a stunning body blow to the already floundering board.

New Zealand lawyers immediately lodged an appeal against the decision but the board was now well out of its depth and, like the ill-fated Soviet liner, sinking rapidly. Apart from NZ$5 million public liability insurance cover, and two or three million dollars in various operating accounts, most of which would probably be swallowed up in legal costs, Port Marlborough New Zealand Ltd, the new port company, was the board's only asset of any significant value left.

Just a year earlier, in February 1988, the board had finally made public the total cost of the Goulden litigation, eventual settlement and associated legal bills. These had amounted to NZ$867,595. Incredibly, in spite of the deep trouble they were in, the board refused to admit any fault, either unfairness in its treatment of Mike Goulden or its actions following the loss of the *Mikhail Lermontov*.

The irony of the situation was not lost on Harbours Tribunal member Brian McClelland. The tribunal had been part-way through the hearings into the Goulden sacking when the *Mikhail Lermontov* sank. When the hearing resumed, Don Jamison continued giving evidence on behalf of the Marlborough Harbour Board, and suggested the manager, Mike Goulden, was incompetent.

Brian McClelland said he thought it was astounding for a pilot who had "single-handedly sunk the biggest ship in peace time since the *Titanic*" to suggest someone else was incompetent.

At a regular board meeting in May 1989, chairman Bruno Dalliessi did however admit the litigation in Australia was the most serious issue that the board had faced. It was an equally astonishing statement because no other New Zealand local authority had ever faced such a formidable prospect.

Dalliessi told the meeting the board would need the support of everyone in the province but still refused to release anything but the barest of details of what he wanted that support for. He had just returned from 17 days in Australia, attending the court hearings. Apart from the few general details already published in Australian and New Zealand newspapers, Dalliessi would say only that he was "very hopeful a satisfactory result would be achieved by the board". He then closed the meeting to the public to make a full report to the board behind closed doors.

The Marlborough community was now thoroughly frustrated by the lack of information about the board's dealings with Mike Goulden, the sinking of the *Mikhail Lermontov*, and the subsequent legal battles in Australia. Letters to the editors of both *The Marlborough Express* and *The Dominion* newspapers suggested that a growing number of people no longer cared if the board won or lost in the Australian court.

If they were not going to be told what was going on, they simply wanted the board abolished and forgotten as soon as possible. Other members of the community still clamoured for a full public enquiry into all the board's affairs. Such was the depth of polarised opinion that a few remained loyal to the board throughout the battles, even though they were as uninformed as anyone else.

On the surface the board appeared to be preparing for a lengthy period of international litigation. Some members even appeared to be enjoying the notoriety. It was to be their last defiant gesture before the board, the last in the country, was abolished. The reality, however, was that it faced major difficulties in successfully defending the charges.

But the board was still intent on finding some way of blaming the loss of the ship on the Russian master, irrespective of the pilot's role. If the sinking could be even in part blamed on Captain Vorobyov, it would reduce the board's share of the loss.

It was against this background that Blenheim lawyer Peter Radich, now acting for the harbour board, contacted a professional diver. Alan Perano had gained a reputation as one of the best in the business. He had worked in many parts of the world, generally on oil rigs and on a number of dangerous salvage missions. Alan's Italian family had arrived in the Marlborough Sounds in the middle of the 19th century at the height of the New Zealand shore-based whaling industry. The Sounds were as familiar as his own backyard.

Peter Radich wanted the diver to join a survey team who were going out to inspect both the now two-year-old wreck on the bottom of Port Gore, and the surrounding sea floor. In particular the harbour board wanted to know if the *Mikhail Lermontov's* anchors had been prepared for lowering or if they were still secured to the winches. If they had not been prepared for lowering, it would indicate the Russian captain could not have stopped the ship from drifting into deep water before she went down, and could therefore be held at least partly to blame for the sinking. Alan Perano was also asked to inspect the reef at Waihi Point near the Baker homestead where, it was rumoured, the ship had struck well before it reached Cape Jackson.

There was no use diving at Waihi Point, Alan said, as any marks left by the ship, if she had struck there, would have long been covered over with the prolific marine growth on the rocky bottom in the two years since the tragedy. Had there been a full public enquiry in the weeks following the sinking, any marks left by a ship would have been still visible, he told them.

The team then sailed around into Port Gore and the surveyors calculated where the cruise ship had first hit the sandy bottom. Photographs taken on the night of the sinking showed how deep in the water the bow of the stricken ship had been when it struck the sand bar. They also located the building on the beach which the Russian master had steered his ship towards just before it ran aground. They gave Alan Perano a compass heading to follow from the building and he set off from the beach along the gently sloping bottom.

About thirty metres out he found a drop of about a metre and then a further section of gently sloping sandy bottom. When he reached the depth calculated as being where the ship had hit he began searching. Soon he found deep gouges and furrows in the sand left by the bow of the ship as it nudged its 20,000 tonnes into the soft sand and then began drifting north-eastwards.

If the anchors had been dropped at this stage, the ship, he said, "would have held at about 100 yards from the beach, and in only about 40 feet of water". This of course would have saved her, although there would still have been dangers for the elderly passengers as they tried to get ashore.

Out in the deep water the *Mikhail Lermontov* lay over on her starboard side as if covering the fatal wound in her flank against the muddy bottom. On her exposed port side two large rips in the hull, about 30 metres back from the bow, could be clearly seen, indicating the ship had been holed on both sides. Moving carefully across the deck, Alan Perano easily found the heavy anchors which had been released from their securing clamps in readiness for lowering. Even without power, the Russian master could have dropped his anchors anywhere he wanted to.

The harbour board now could not show that the master was unprepared to drop anchor, and, without a formal enquiry, they were unable to find out why he had not anchored his sinking ship when he had the opportunity. He had told the Ponsford Enquiry he wanted to get closer to the beach before letting passengers off.

Court proceedings began in Sydney, and the Marlborough Harbour Board was represented by its counsel.

Proceedings had gone on for some time when the question of possible settlement arose. Lawyers for both sides then set about negotiating rather than slugging it out in court. The settlement was to be on the basis of "no liability admitted and no details made public".

For reasons which never became clear, the Russians had appeared to throw in the towel. It may be that within the Soviet Union at that time it was thought better to accept the economic impact of the loss of the ship rather than have a prolonged public hearing in a western-style judicial system where questions would be asked and would have to be answered.

After prolonged negotiation, the harboard board paid the last of its financial reserves, about NZ$2.5 million, to the Baltic Shipping Company for the loss of the ship and all other claims. The settlement emptied the board's bank balance, and left it with a deficit of an unknown amount. This was probably met by the Marlborough District Council.

The final settlement to individual passengers has never been revealed.

The Marlborough Harbour Board, the last such board left in the country, then went out of existence. Port Marlborough New Zealand was transferred to the Marlborough District Council and the neighbouring Kaikoura District Council in 1989. The statutory functions of the board, and the last of its staff, were also transferred to the Marlborough District

Council.

New Zealand's last harbour board, after several decades of useful and profitable operation, thus passed into history disgraced and with its coffers empty..

Similar claims for compensation against Don Jamison were eventually dropped, probably as part of the agreement between the board and the shipping company. Part of the negotiated settlement was that all details would be kept secret, and only those directly involved were supposed to know what those details were.

The Marlborough District Council has a file on the saga, a file which has never been opened to the public. And it was the public, the people of Marlborough, who, in the final analysis, paid all the bills.

Epilogue

THE *Mikhail Lermontov* was eventually abandoned by the Baltic Shipping Company, and still lies in 40 metres of water at Port Gore.

Her lifeboats can be seen in various places around New Zealand. One sits outside a Picton shopping mall, where it serves as a place for shoppers to enjoy a cup of coffee. Another has been adapted as a ship broker's office in nearby Havelock harbour at the head of Pelorus Sound.

The ship herself continues to be visited by recreational divers, some of whom have returned dozens of times to the wreck.

When they returned to Russia, Captain Vorobyov and his senior officers faced a second and much sterner enquiry, this time by Soviet Government officials. Their enquiry found the principal cause of the loss of the *Mikhail Lermontov* was the decision by the New Zealand pilot, Captain Don Jamison to navigate the ship through the Cape Jackson Passage.

Some blame was apportioned to Captain Vorobyov who, the enquiry said, should have kept closer supervision of the pilot, particularly in view of his concerns about the pilot's taking the ship too close to the shore at least twice prior to the grounding. He was officially reprimanded, permanently stripped of his sea-going qualifications and given shore duties.

After the collapse of the Soviet Union in 1991, however, Captain Vorobyov returned to sea-going duties and now commands a freight ship. He still lives in Moscow.

Chief navigator Sergey Stepanishchev, who was on the bridge at the time of the grounding, was given a four-year suspended prison sentence, four years' probation and fined 20,000 roubles (about NZ$23,000 in 1986). The enquiry found he should have countermanded the pilot's order to the helmsman, the order which sent the ship through the passage to its doom.

Captain Jamison returned to his job as harbourmaster with the Marlborough Harbour Board until it was abolished in 1989 but never resumed pilotage duties. He now commands the livestock ferry, *Suilivan*, operating between Picton and Wellington. He has never spoken publicly about the tragedy.

Captain John Reedman, master of the gas tanker *Tarihiko*, was awarded the Queen's Service Medal. Captain John Brew of the Cook Strait ferry *Arahura* was presented with a silver salver and his crew received silver tankards from Soviet authorities for their work in the rescue of the ship's passengers.

In addition to refrigeration engineer Parvee Zagliadimov, who died when the ship went down, three other people have since lost their lives on the *Mikhail Lermontov*. All were experienced divers.

The first fatality was Erica Jane Low of Wellington who was diving with a group in May 1987 when she disappeared. Her body was found near the swimming pool in October the following year.

The second tragedy occurred in January 1989 when 40-year-old Barry Leslie Evans of Christchurch apparently got lost inside the ship. He had been diving with a companion in the restaurant area and became separated soon after they decided to return to the surface. He was later found unconscious and with his mask off, and was taken quickly to the surface but efforts to revive him failed.

The third accident was in July 1989 when 19-year-old Martin Greig of Blenheim became separated from his diving group. It was his 21st dive on the ship, and he had been down only about 10 minutes. His body was not recovered.

Of the sea of rumours which erupted immediately after the loss of the *Mikhail Lermontov*, a few still circulate. Most persistent is that it was a deliberate act to cover up Soviet KGB or American CIA spy activities, or to bring New Zealand to heel over its prohibition of nuclear-powered and armed ships in territorial waters. Accusations are also still made that the Ponsford Enquiry was a sham with a foregone conclusion, under secret directions from the New Zealand Government.

Perhaps the most damaging rumour of all is that both the Russian master and the pilot were drunk. Incredible as it may seem, many still hold that view. In their testimony to the Ponsford Enquiry, both men strongly refuted that suggestion. If such a serious breach of seamanship had indeed occurred, there would have been indications in the testimony of other senior officers who were on the bridge that night. While it could be argued that Russian officers might cover for their captain, it is unlikely they would have told lies to cover for the pilot - the man they blamed for the loss of their ship.

Although there was no cross-examination of witnesses at the enquiry, and there are several significant contradictions in their evidence, there is no evidence whatsoever that anyone on the bridge was drunk.

Not a single rumour has stood up under investigation but, as with all dramatic and tragic events, theories will survive and grow for as long as there are people to repeat them. Most if not all of the rumours would have been laid to rest if there had been a full public enquiry into the loss of the *Mikhail Lermontov*. The decision not to hold that enquiry was just one of many decisions, both before and after the sinking, that still raise questions many years later.

The ghost of the *Mikhail Lermontov* still haunts the dreams of those who survived her sinking, and the imaginations of those who were not even on board that terrible night. It is certain that people will pick over her bones and disturb her resting place for many years to come.

Some literary critics believe the revolutionary poet and writer Mikhail Lermontov would have equalled Tolstoi and Pushkin in Russian literature had he lived longer. He died far from his Moscow home while fighting a duel on the edge of a cliff, and taking unnecessary risks too close to the edge.
The cruise ship Mikhail Lermontov *sank in Port Gore, New Zealand, far from her Russian home port, while taking unnecessary risks too close to the shore.*

Bibliography

The Alexander Turnbull Library, Wellington, New Zealand (archives) including Bellingshausen and d'Urville

The Australian Police Journal
The Dominion newspaper
The Marlborough Express newspaper
Hansard, New Zealand
The New Zealand Listener magazine
North and South magazine
Television New Zealand
The Enigma of the Mikhail Lermontov, Michael Guerin
New Zealand Geographic magazine, April 1999

Glossary

Aft: stern or rear of a ship.
Ballast: weight in a ship, often water, to aid stability.
Bilge keels: fins attached to the bottom of a ship either side of the central keel.
Bow thruster: enclosed propeller, used to push the bow to port or starboard during low-speed operations.
Bridge: central control area of a ship.
Conned: controlled; usually of a ship at sea.
List: lean to one side.
LPG tanker: Liquid petroleum gas-carrying ship.
Making water: water is entering accidentally.
Master: captain.
Mate: Senior officer, subordinate to the captain.
Ngati Kuia: a New Zealand Maori tribe.
Pilot: master mariner who navigates a ship in and out of ports, or in dangerous waters.
Port: left side of a ship.
Rangitane: a New Zealand Maori tribe.
Sounding line: thin rope with a weight attached and marks for measuring the depth of water.
Starboard: right side of a ship.
Tender: motorised launch carried for general use and emergencies.
VHF radio: Very High Frequency radio.
Way: momentum or powered movement of a ship.